FLYING HIGHER

FLYING HIGHER

by

Rick Godwin

CREATION
HOUSE

FLYING HIGHER by Rick Godwin
Published by Creation House
Strang Communications Company
600 Rinehart Road
Lake Mary, Florida 32746
Web site: http://www.creationhouse.com

Unless otherwise noted, all Scripture quotations are from the New King James Version of the Bible. Copyright © 1979, 1980, 1982 by Thomas Nelson, Inc., publishers. Used by permission.

Scripture quotations marked NIV are from the Holy Bible, New International Version. Copyright © 1973, 1978, 1984, International Bible Society. Used by permission.

Scripture quotations marked KJV are from the King James Version of the Bible.

Scripture quotations marked NLT are from the Holy Bible, New Living Translation, copyright © 1996. Used by permission of Tyndale House Publishers, Inc., Wheaton, IL 60189. All rights reserved.

Scripture quotations marked NAS are from the New American Standard Bible. Copyright © 1960, 1962, 1963, 1968, 1971, 1972, 1973, 1975, 1977 by the Lockman Foundation. Used by permission.

Scripture quotations marked NRSV are from the New Revised Standard Version of the Bible. Copyright © 1989 by the Division of Christian Education of the National Council of the Churches of Christ in the USA. Used by permission.

Scripture quotations marked TLB are from The Living Bible. Copyright © 1971. Used by permission of Tyndale House Publishers, Inc., Wheaton, IL 60189. All rights reserved.

Scripture quotations marked CEV are from the Contemporary English Version, copyright © 1995 by the America Bible Society. Used by permission.

Library of Congress Cataloging-in-Publication Data
Godwin, Rick.
    Flying higher / Rick Godwin.
        p. cm.
    ISBN: 0-88419-568–6 (pbk.)
    1. Christian life. I. Title.
BV4501.2.G595 1999
248.4—dc21

98-55357
CIP

9 0 1 2 3 4 5 6 BBG 8 7 6 5 4 3 2 1
Printed in the United States of America

Acknowledgments

I would like to acknowledge and express my personal thanks to some great men of God who have been tremendous blessings in my life. My deepest appreciation to:

- Kevin Conner, Victoria, Australia

- Bob Mumford, Raleigh, North Carolina

- Ralph Mahoney, founder of the mission organization World Map

I believe this book is just one of many ways in which their mentoring has influenced my life and ministry.

Contents

Foreword

PLEASE PASTOR, CAN YOU TELL ME HOW I CAN know that it is God's leading in this decision?"

That question, or some form of it, is perhaps one of the most frequently asked questions of pastors today. People are confused about "the voice of God," which really means they don't understand the methods that God uses to confirm His promptings and leadings in our lives. God actually wants to be involved in all of our decision making. He would like us to be led by Him every step of the way.

This book is not just theory. Pastor Rick Godwin emphasizes the scriptural truth that God's guidance will never contradict the Word of God. Too many Christians base God's guidance on their own circumstantial evidence, the most deceptive means of making a decision.

Flying Higher is not just about the ways that people are missing God's direction. It points out and explains the different ways by which God leads us, and how to line His leadings up with our own decision-making processes. Rick Godwin, one of America's great leaders and communicators, has a remarkably wonderful way of painting visual word pictures and creating analogies and illustrations that really hit home and leave a lasting impression.

I know this book will bless every reader as it has those who have heard this teaching in various forms—either in live meetings or on audiocassette. Now, this book provides the entire dimension of this teaching in one handy, easy-to-absorb and easy-to-use volume.

I believe that everyone who reads this book, takes it to heart and applies the principles therein will grow in maturity and sensitivity. As they realize they can follow God's leading to maximize His purposes in their lives, they will be a blessing to everyone around them and to the very heart of God.

—TOMMY BARNETT
PASTOR, PHOENIX FIRST ASSEMBLY OF GOD

Rick Godwin has never been one to settle for apathy, mediocrity or ignorance. His noncompromising approach inspires one to strive for excellence and expect supernatural results, no matter what situation you are in. I've always admired his incredible ability to dig deep into God's Word and pull out profound truths, making revelation knowledge sound like simple common sense. His teachings have had a powerful impact on my life and have inspired me to strive for a higher level in my personal walk with God. The bottom line is to understand God's Word, apply it and see it work! Let me warn you, after reading this book you will have no excuses left but to become an A-level Christian.

—Brian Houston
President, Hillsongs Australia
National Superintendent,
Assemblies of God in Australia

Introduction

YOU'RE FLYING ACROSS THE COUNTRY TO VISIT relatives. Because they live in a remote area of Montana, you're forced to conclude your journey on a commuter flight. After you're well on your way, the flight attendant bursts through the door to the cockpit, screaming, "I think the pilot just died of a heart attack! Does anyone here know how to fly an airplane?"

None of the twenty passengers on board know how, but you have experienced playing one of those flight simulator games on the computer, so you volunteer your services.

Entering the cockpit, you are greeted by a vast array of levers, buttons, gauges and gadgets. You realize that it's one thing to fly an airplane on a computer, but the simulation is worlds apart from the real thing.

Overwhelmed, you survey the instrument panel. What do you do? Which buttons do you push? Which levers do you pull? One wrong move could prove disastrous. You wonder how even a pilot could ever learn to fly this thing.

Sometimes deciphering God's will feels a lot like trying to fly that airplane. Throughout our lives we face myriad decisions, each of which can, and does, radically alter our lives. Just as the pilot's heart attack affected the passengers, the consequences of our decisions directly affect those "going along for the ride": family members, friends, business associates and brothers and sisters in Christ. Once we are flying with our decisions, it is difficult to turn around and return to our place of origin. Plus, we easily become fearful of an ugly "crash and burn."

When facing major decisions, we often feel overwhelmed by the options that lie in front of us, just as the simulator game player did when faced with the actual airplane instrument panel. What should I do with my life? What college should I attend? Should I change careers? Is this the person I should marry? Is this the right time to have children? Can I succeed if I go into business for myself? Should I sell my house now or later? Should I plant a church here or there? Should I make a major purchase or wait? The decisions we face are endless.

One voice tells us to go one direction. Another voice tells us to go another direction.

To which voice do we listen?

Fortunately, God has given us a guidance system for navigating our way through decision-making, even when the weather is turbulent. Unfortunately, many well-meaning believers understand God's guidance system about as well as the computer game player who knew nothing about flying a real airplane. Unless you're acquainted with the guidance system you have been given, your flight will not only be bumpy but also potentially disastrous.

Many people's idea of guidance from God is like that of a certain businessman who didn't spend much time in the Word. One day he prayed, "Lord, I need a word of guidance." He picked up his dusty Bible off the coffee table, closed his eyes, let it flop open and put his finger down on the page. When he opened his eyes, he noticed that he was pointing to the word *wheat,* so he called his stockbroker and invested a large sum of money on wheat futures. Within weeks he was reaping quite a prosperous return on his investment.

After a while wheat began declining, so he decided he needed another word from God. Once again he dusted off his Bible, closed his eyes, let it flop open and put his finger on the page. This time he was pointing to the word *oil.* He asked his stockbroker to liquidate all of his wheat stock and invest in oil reserves. Again he prospered, adding to the fortune he had already made.

When the price of oil took a nosedive, instead of cutting his losses, he decided to ride it out. In the end, he lost everything. Devastated, he met with a lawyer friend who advised him about the different forms of bankruptcy. The idea of bankruptcy shocked the man. "I don't believe God would guide me into bankruptcy."

"Well, you had better get a word from God because you're in big trouble," his friend counseled him.

The man returned home and said, "I need another word from God." He picked up his trusty, dusty Bible, closed his eyes, let it fall open and jammed his finger down on the page. When he opened his eyes, he read, "Chapter 11."

Believe it or not, that is the way many believers seek God's will. Because of impatience, immaturity or ignorance, they settle for a Bible "crap shoot" rather than taking the time to learn God's guidance system. Other Christians call their psychic "friend," who's much more interested in their money than in being their friend. Some call in to radio talk shows, where they ask people who know nothing about them or the ways of God for advice. Still others decide to go it alone and end up in a hole with no one to pull them out.

But our heavenly Father has something far better for us than those options. God has made available to every Christian a guidance system that is both simple and complex: simple because it is based in Scripture; complex because, without a knowledge of God's simple truths, it can be misleading.

The foundation in our study of God's guidance rests on Romans 8:14: "For as many as are led by the Spirit of God, these are sons of God." The sons of God—all believers in Jesus Christ—are *led* by the Spirit of God. If we belong to God, then God promised that He is *already* leading us.

Failing to follow where God leads is usually due to one of two reasons: rebellion or recognition. If you are in rebellion and don't care to follow God's leading even when you recognize it, my book *Exposing Witchcraft in the Church* may be helpful. If you would like to improve your competence in recognizing *how* God leads, then this book is just what you need.

Here you will discover seven principles of God's guidance that can keep you on course, out of error, out of destruction and out of danger so that you can finish your life avoiding "crash-and-burn" decisions. Best of all, these principles not only will help you to avoid making bad decisions, but they will also help you to make good, godly decisions.

Much like all the dials, buttons and switches on the instrument panel in the cockpit of an airplane, God's biblical principles each have a purpose in guiding us toward His will for us. Individually, each principle gives a partial and incomplete glimpse of how God leads. But when considered alongside of other biblical principles of God's guidance, they give a more complete picture of His direction for our lives.

My prayer for you is that you will learn how to better recognize the voice of the Good Shepherd when making decisions. May God bless you as you discover His divine guidance system.

≈

On August 31, 1983 a Korean Air Lines (KAL) Boeing 747 departed from Anchorage, Alaska, on its way to Seoul. Soon after its departure, the commercial aircraft deviated from its planned route and ultimately ended up in protected Soviet airspace. Approaching the Sakhalin Island, the plane was intercepted by Russian military fighters. About a half an hour later, the commercial aircraft was hit by at least one air-to-air missile fired by the Soviets. The Boeing crashed into the sea, killing twenty-three crew members and 246 passengers on board.

After the disaster, investigators speculated that the navigational system for the flight had been incorrectly programmed and that this pilot never knew where he was when he was shot down.*

In the very same way God has given us wonderful, powerful systems through which to navigate our choices in life. But if we do not employ these systems, or if we use them incorrectly, we're liable to suffer a similar fate as the Korean pilot.

≈

---

* Compiled from information found on the Harro Ranter/Aviation Safety Web Pages, updated 5 July 1998, copyright © 1996–98.

Part I:

Taking Off
Safely

≈

1

Learning to Be
Led by the Spirit

HOW WOULD YOU LIKE TO DRIVE YOUR CAR without the benefit of seeing through your front windshield? Driving with no front vision would be a terrifying experience. Without the luxury of vision every turn in the road and every passing car would present new challenges to the invincibility of your vehicle—perhaps even your life. Even if cars were equipped with radars, video screens and the like, it is doubtful that most people would choose this equipment over the ability to see for themselves.

However, if you were flying an airplane using just your eyesight to navigate, the results could be disastrous. Flying by sight would most likely be your secondary method of navigation. The primary method, especially in turbulent times, would be flying by instruments.

FLYING BY SIGHT HAS ITS LIMITS

In the same way that every bike rider begins with training wheels, all pilots begin flight training by learning to fly by sight. Although it soon becomes second nature, flying by sight limits what the aviator is able or authorized to do. The pilot without an Instrument Flight Rating (IFR) is required by law to fly only under conditions in which he or she is able to see in front of the airplane. By flying at lower altitudes and beneath a cloud cover, the pilot is able to identify landmarks, such as train tracks, roads and rivers, using them to locate the plane's present position and intended destination. Though flying in darkness is allowed without an IFR, at night the pilot is limited by his inability to see approaching aircraft, radio towers, power lines and other landmarks.

Encountering a storm miles from an airport is a disaster waiting to happen. Because the pilot is neither authorized nor equipped to fly above the clouds (beyond his ability to fly by sight), he has to fly close to the storm, possibly subjecting the plane to lightning, ice on the wings, hail, severe turbulence and a host of other dangers.

Flying by sight *through* storm clouds is dangerous because clouds are deceptive. In storms pilots have been known to fly without regard to their instrument panel, only to emerge from clouds either flying upside down or going the wrong way. What the pilot saw with his eyes actually led him in the wrong direction. Worst of all, in a cloud the pilot can collide with another plane and never know what hit him.

Earning an instrument rating is a major accomplishment for any pilot. The Instrument Flight Rating licenses the pilot to commandeer aircraft at higher altitudes, in darkness and in inclement weather by utilizing artificial means of sight—radar, monitors, gauges and other flight instruments.

Earning the IFR demands a measure of faith and discipline because the pilot must learn to "fly blind." Rather than relying on sight, the pilot is forced to depend upon the guidance system present within the airplane. Flying by instruments allows the pilot to navigate safely around storms and through fog or heavy cloud cover that he may encounter.

The same is true of every believer.

All too often, believers make rash decisions in the middle of a storm based on what they see. And without an understanding of God's guidance system, they experience disastrous results. Had they learned the freedom of flying by instruments—that is, being led by the Spirit—the outcome may have been vastly different.

WHAT DOES IT MEAN TO BE LED BY THE SPIRIT?

Paul wrote, "For as many as are led by the Spirit of God, these are sons of God" (Rom. 8:14). Some Christians relate being led by the

3

Spirit to Luke Skywalker's experience in the movie *Star Wars*. During his training to become a Jedi knight, Luke put on a helmet that prevented him from seeing. Then, relying on "the Force"—an ethereal, spirit-like energy field—he tried to strike a target with his galactic sword that was bobbing around in midair. As his training was completed, Obi-Wan Kenobi, his mentor, advised young Luke Skywalker, "Your eyes deceive you. Don't trust them."

To some people, being led by the Spirit means relying on that same kind of ethereal spiritual energy. Just as every nuance in the wind alters the direction of a kite in the air, the Spirit-led believer is led to and fro as a spiritual wanderer by the wind of the Spirit, or so some believe.

Others envision Spirit-led believers as different from normal people. They must have wild looks in their eyes and respond to voices that no one else hears or understands. This description of the Spirit-led believer does not correspond with what God's Word really says.

Paul encouraged the believers in the church at Corinth to "walk by faith, not by sight" (2 Cor. 5:7). Being led by the Spirit means recognizing the various promptings of the Holy Spirit, then walking by them rather than by what we see.

TWO HINDRANCES TO BEING LED BY THE SPIRIT

Most believers tend toward one extreme or

4

the other when seeking to be led by the Spirit: human rationale or mysticism. Each extreme gives the believer only a partial glimpse into God's guidance.

Human rationale: Playing it safe

Relying on human rationale means that we must never move outside the realm of what is seen, what is known and what is logical; all questions must be answered, every door must be opened and all risk must be eliminated before moving out "in faith." Actually, living like this precludes us from moving out in faith. How can faith be involved when no faith is required?

A man named John yearned to plant a church. An associate pastor, he was good at starting new ministries and building a ministry team. Members of his congregation had recently asked if he had ever considered planting a church. He even had a vision that he felt God had given him for this new endeavor. "If God wants me to plant a church," John replied to his inquirers, "then He's just going to have to open up the right doors."

His home church offered to provide a covering and its blessing should he decide to plant a new church. John's wife even offered to work part time to supplement their income. But despite the fact that he sensed God urging him to go, he never followed through because he didn't know anyone in the city where the church would have been planted. That was the one uncertainty that remained. Since John couldn't neatly tie up all the loose ends, he didn't move out, settling instead for a situation that left him unfulfilled and unchallenged.

For many the biggest hurdle to being Spirit-led is the leap of faith that is required. Believing in One we cannot see and trusting in a God who defies human logic is too great a chasm for some people to cross. These people require that all their ducks be lined up in a row before they move out. Unfortunately, the ducks seldom line up just right, so they rarely move.

However, Paul reminds us, "We walk by *faith*, not by sight" (2 Cor. 5:7, emphasis added). Furthermore, the Bible states that without faith it's impossible to please God (Heb. 11:6). Faith is sometimes spelled r-i-s-k. That's a calculated risk, not a presumptuous risk. There's a big difference.

A calculated risk means counting the cost before making the jump. A presumptuous risk means making the jump without fully counting the cost. The goal of this book is to help you take godly, calculated, yet faith-based risks—without falling.

At the same time taking a risk is not necessarily equal to walking in faith. A decision that is devoid of personal reliance upon God is not a faith-based risk. For John, a risky but poor decision would have been to move his family without running the idea by his spiritual leaders and mentors, without prayer and without a conscious act of seeking God's direction. Living by faith means prayerfully involving God every step of the way.

Mysticism: The unseeable, the unknowable and the uncertain

The other extreme that is a hindrance to receiving God's guidance is mysticism—being led by the unseeable, the unknowable and the uncertain. People caught in this extreme often say they "feel led." They cloak their attempts to push their will onto others with the almost threatening introduction, "God said." Often, people who say they are "being led" are just putting up smoke screens for their own selfishness and subjective feelings.

Many people fall into one of these two extremes when deciding whom to marry. Those who live by human rationale give God a shopping list of what they want in a spouse: brown hair, blue eyes, muscular, successful in business. Sometimes the list is so specific and idealistic that their potential mate could not even exist! When a godly person having many of those qualities, but not all of them, comes along, the spouse-seeker rejects him because he doesn't fit the exact description.

People who respond mystically act just the opposite. Let's say Chris spots a young, single woman at church who really charges his jets. Jenna looks good, she has an infectious smile and, best of all, she raises her hands during worship. For Chris, who happens to be on the rebound from a previous relationship, that pretty much meets all the criteria on his list. After observing Jenna for a few weeks at church, Chris finally musters up the courage—or the audacity—to meet her.

"While we were worshiping this morning," Chris confides to his new potential prayer partner, "God quickened my spirit to pray for you. Is there anything I can agree with you for in prayer?" (This is what you call a classic Christian pick-up line!) Jenna shares a few menial items with him, but Chris, digging for more information, invites her to lunch.

After a few more dates Chris has a further confession to make: "Jenna, I don't know about you, but I feel God may have more in store for us than just praying together." You can pretty well figure out how the story concludes.

Some Christians confuse being led by their hormones with being led by the Spirit. They get married, and then, when the honeymoon ends and the relationship must rest on more than feelings, the marriage falters. After realizing where they went wrong, some Christians are even brazen enough to say God is leading them *out* of the marriage— sometimes even to a different person. This propensity toward mysticism then becomes a license for leaving a spouse.

People who follow their subjective feelings under the guise of "being led by the Spirit" are disasters waiting to happen.

THE PRINCIPLE OF MULTIPLE WITNESSES

So, how do we make godly, balanced decisions?

I believe the key to God's guidance system lies in the principle of multiple witnesses.

In Deuteronomy, Moses established the process by which a person would be judged: "Whoever is deserving of death shall be put to death on the testimony of two or three witnesses; he shall not be put to death on the testimony of one witness" (17:6). The word of one person was not enough evidence to establish guilt. The courts of justice in the Western world still reflect this principle today. Likewise, the court sessions we hold in our minds when we are trying to make decisions also require the testimony of two or three witnesses.

These are the seven witnesses—or principles—that God has given us and that we'll explore throughout this book: inner conviction, the Word of God, prophetic corroboration, godly counsel, circumstantial evidence, the peace of God and provision. We need the testimony—the agreement—of several of these witnesses to make godly decisions. In this way subjectivity is eliminated. The bigger the decision, the greater the risk, the more varied the witnesses you want lined up.

God gives us a variety of ways to discern His will, but He never intended for us to employ one to the neglect of the others. People stumble most often when they give one principle greater weight than the others. Overemphasis on godly counsel or the peace of God or prophetic corroboration opens a person to great risk. Books have been written

9

on each of these seven principles, and from these we can get the impression that one or the other of the principles is the key to knowing the whole will of God. But relying on one witness can preclude you from safety and success.

Let me note here that you do not need the witness of all seven principles to move out with God. This may happen occasionally, but you will not always receive a prophetic word, for instance, to confirm your inner conviction, your peace or the word God has given you from Scripture.

NEVER VIOLATE A WITNESS

Proverbs 3:6 says, "In all your ways acknowledge Him, and He shall direct your paths." Though we don't need all seven witnesses, we should never make decisions that violate or contradict any one of the seven witnesses. We can't violate any part of the Word of God and still be doing the will of God. If He doesn't give you a green light, then don't move. You could have a green light in one move. Don't be frightened. God isn't frightened. He knows how to confirm. So, acknowledge Him in *all* of your ways.

I can't tell you how many leaders I have known who felt they had a mandate from God, so they failed to see the red lights God set up in front of them. Godly counselors may have advised them against making a move or perhaps the provision wasn't there, but they remained undeterred. In the end they returned shattered, bruised and broken.

God is big, God is secure and God is fair. He's going to make sure you clearly know what to do and have all your bases covered when He sends you into something new. That doesn't mean you can eliminate risk altogether, because faith is filled with some risk. But it will be well calculated because you won't be violating any of the seven witnesses. You will be flying by instruments, being led in faith by the Spirit of God.

Questions for Reflection

1. Think of a time when you were led to make a leap of faith. How did you know it was the right thing to do? What happened?

_____

_____

_____

_____

2. Do you lean toward an extreme—human rationale or mysticism—when making decisions? Why?

_____

_____

_____

_____

3. In what ways do you believe that applying the principle of multiple witnesses will give you stability and calmness in decision-making?

_____

_____

_____

_____

_____

2

Overcoming Obstacles to God's Guidance

THE MOST POTENTIALLY PERILOUS MOMENTS IN flight involve the takeoff and landing of the airplane. During these times the vast majority of accidents takes place.

Weather conditions can prevent a safe and successful takeoff: for example, heat and humidity, wind shear and freezing rain. Yet the pilot may be oblivious to these environmental factors without the assistance of air traffic control. Without clear communication between the two, the pilot is risking the lives of everyone on board.

Even while the plane is still on the ground the pilot must rely on those around him. Assistance from ground control—those funny-looking guys with ear protectors and orange flashlights standing beside the jet—enables the pilot to back up from the air terminal without hitting the ramp or other parked airplanes. Air traffic control then dictates to the pilot the path to the runway. Should the pilot misunderstand or fail to heed the air traffic controller's directives, the pilot might unknowingly attempt a takeoff on a runway intended for landings.

Communication, therefore, is crucial, and a lack of it is a recipe for disaster even before the flight begins.

OBSTACLES TO HEARING GOD'S VOICE

Just as the pilot needs to hear from the air traffic controllers, we need to hear from God. Without clear communication from God in the midst of making a major decision, the believer endangers himself and others.

Seven obstacles hinder us from hearing God's voice clearly and discerning His direction for our lives. Failure to overcome any one of these is like trying to maneuver your airplane from the terminal to the runway without ground or air support.

Obstacle #1: Being lost

The first obstacle that prevents people from clearly hearing God's voice is *being lost*—not giving the controls of your life to Jesus Christ.

A few years ago a popular bumper sticker read, "God is my co-pilot." But God's Word tells us He wants us out of the cockpit so He can be in complete control. He wants our bumper stickers to read, "God *alone* is my pilot."

16

In the first and foremost of the Ten Commandments, God reveals that He is a jealous God and there are to be no other gods besides Him (Exod. 20:3–5). In fact, He goes so far as to tell us that His name *is* Jealous (Exod. 34:14).

All too often, however, our god is the person in the mirror. When we seek to please ourselves, when we're looking out only for number one, we fashion ourselves (in our own eyes) into the likeness of God. The Bible tells us that is sin.

The biggest barrier that separates us from a perfect and sinless God is our sin. In Isaiah, God tells us, "But your iniquities have separated you from your God; and your sins have hidden His face from you, so that He will not hear" (59:2). If you haven't given your life to Jesus Christ, you can pray all day long for direction from God, but He won't even hear your prayer. The only prayer He is obligated to hear and heed before you become a Christian is the prayer of repentance, in which you confess your need for God to remove the barrier of sin that separates you from Him.

When Jesus, the Son of God, came to earth, He showed us the way to know God the Father. Jesus declared, "I am the way, the truth, and the life. No one comes to the Father except through Me" (John 14:6). As we yield ourselves to Jesus Christ, ask Him to remove our sins and put Him in control of our lives, we cross the barrier that separated us from God.

Once we belong to Jesus, we are given

Jesus-headphones and Jesus-contact lenses that enable us to hear His voice and see His guidance. Jesus, our Good Shepherd, then says of us:

> The sheep hear his voice; and he calls his own sheep by name and leads them out. And when he brings out his own sheep, he goes before them; and the sheep follow him, for they know his voice. Yet they will by no means follow a stranger, but will flee from him, for they do not know the voice of strangers.
> —John 10:3–5

Sheep know the voice of their shepherd. It's the birthright of every believer to hear God's voice; every believer has the capacity to do this. Jesus said that the sheep follow Him because they recognize His voice.

In Australia, where sheep outnumber people, I once observed a shepherd at work with his sheep. The sheep were doing their own thing, grazing and doing what sheep do best. If I had raised my voice to call them, they wouldn't have responded. If you aren't the shepherd, you can make all the noise you want to get the sheep to follow you, but they won't budge an inch. But the moment the old shepherd got out of his truck and lifted his voice, they responded immediately, following the voice of their master. You can't fake out sheep.

A lot of people want answers to their problems—they want marriages healed and finances straightened out—but they don't want to be saved and to become part of the flock. As long as they remain lost sheep, God has no obligation to speak to them. Out of love and grace He often does, but He has no obligation to do so.

Obstacle #2: Not being Spirit-filled

The second obstacle to hearing God's voice and recognizing His direction is *not being Spirit-filled.* A person can go to heaven and still not be filled with the Holy Spirit.

At one time in my Christian life, I used to say, "When I got saved, I got everything." And in a technical sense, I did. When Israel stood on the east bank of the Jordan, looking across the river into the Promised Land, God said to Joshua and the people, "I have given you the land; here is the deed, paid in full."

Now, if they had been like many Christians, they would have lined up all the way down the east bank and said, "It's all ours," yet never set a foot in it. Legally, it *was* theirs, but experientially, they hadn't possessed it yet.

In a real sense, all Christians are given the Holy Spirit at salvation. At the same time, however, the power of the Holy Spirit may not yet be released. God has more for the believer than just the indwelling of the Holy Spirit; believers need the Spirit's immersion as well. And that's what baptism means—"to immerse."

Beginning in Acts 2, we read about people who are already saved; but once they have

19

been Spirit-filled, they are given not only power to be witnesses but also a divine capacity to move in the gifts of the Spirit. (For more information on the gifts of the Spirit, read 1 Corinthians 12–14; Romans 12:4–8 and Ephesians 4:7–13.)

For example, when facing a decision, the gift of discernment (one of the gifts of the Spirit) enables me to sense factors regarding my situation that would be impossible for me to know in my natural understanding. Perhaps you're considering a job change when God gives you discernment that your new boss is not nearly what he appears to be. Without the infilling of the Holy Spirit, how would you be able to sense the Holy Spirit's leading or walk in the gifts of the Spirit?

The baptism of the Holy Spirit, then, is the means by which God enlivens *your* spirit so you can move in the power of the *Holy* Spirit.

If you're unsure whether or not you are filled, you probably aren't. In the New Testament people received this baptism through prayer, through the laying on of hands from other Spirit-filled believers, through preaching and through worship (Acts 1:14–2:4; 4:31; 8:17; 9:17; 11:15; Eph. 5:18–19). It's not important how you receive as long as you do receive. So if you feel empty, you need to be filled or refilled. Once you're filled, you'll know it!

Obstacle #3: Pride

The third obstacle that prevents us from knowing God's will is *pride*. Pride is the attitude that declares that *I* know what is best for me, that I choose to whom I will listen. It means being stiff, unteachable, unbendable, unchangeable; it means I won't repent, I won't take responsibility and I know it all.

The Bible tells us in James that "God resists the proud, but gives grace to the humble" (4:6). If I am filled with pride, I find myself fighting God for control of my destiny. On the other hand Psalm 25:9 reveals, "The humble He guides in justice, and the humble He teaches His way." God guides the humble because they are teachable and willing to follow.

Historians tell us that a gigantic iceberg sank the luxury liner *Titanic* off the coast of Newfoundland on April 15, 1912; but really, pride sank that ship. Everything about the *Titanic* breathed opulence and self-sufficiency. It was simply the greatest ship built in human history; it represented the crowning achievement of mankind at that time. But observe Casey Sabella's keen insight into what really sank the *Titanic:*

> The philosophy of [the *Titanic's*] operation including excellence, image, and profit was rooted in self. Pride blinded the minds of nearly everyone on board. God, in His mercy, sent the *Titanic* no less than six messages warning of impending disaster. In each case, and for various reasons, the captain and crew ignored those warnings to their own peril.[1]

21

Six times the crew was warned by surrounding ships that icebergs lay ahead on that dark, moonless night, but the crew was so convinced their ship was unsinkable that they ignored the messages they were given. In much the same way God sends warning signs to avert disaster in our own lives, but when we are controlled by pride, we are unable or unwilling to recognize His voice.

The quickest way to get a word from God and get yourself out of a big mess is to take responsibility and humble yourself. God promises He will guide the humble, but the proud He will cut off from His guidance system, leaving them to their own devices.

Obstacle #4: Self-deception

The fourth obstacle to hearing from God is *self-deception*. James admonishes us, "But be doers of the word and not hearers only, deceiving yourselves" (James 1:22). The Contemporary English Version makes it even more explicit: "Obey God's message! Don't fool yourselves by just listening to it." This passage explains why so many Christians never change.

Often, when we just hear the Word, we think that we're living it. We hear about prayer, we talk about prayer, we talk about talking about prayer; in the process we convince ourselves that we are praying. But we aren't—we're only hearing about prayer or talking about prayer—we're not praying. That's self-deception. We do the same thing with evangelism, loving our neighbor, knowing God—you name it.

James goes on to describe people like this: "For if anyone is a hearer of the word and not a doer, he is like a man observing his natural face in a mirror; for he observes himself, goes away, and immediately forgets what kind of man he was" (vv. 23–24).

When you woke up this morning, chances are you looked in the mirror, brushed your teeth, took a shower, shaved (if you're a man), combed your hair, put on a little makeup (if you're a woman) and maybe some deodorant. You got things in order because the mirror revealed what was wrong. You didn't like what you saw, so you came into agreement with your mirror, and you did something about it.

In the same way many people walk up to the mirror of God's Word and see themselves as God sees them. But then they walk away without doing anything about what they saw.

What amazes me is why so many Christians walk away unchanged from the very tool designed to help them. People have a tendency to build a protective barrier that prevents God's Word from penetrating into them where they need it most. They read God's Word and assume that their responsibility stops right there. People like this find how God's Word applies to everyone else but themselves. And what they discover that does apply, they reject.

God also uses those close to us to reveal

our error. If three people call you a donkey—buy a saddle! Accept your closest friends' observation of you *by faith,* because if you are deceived, you will never see it!

When we approach God for guidance, we need to be prepared to do whatever He directs us to do instead of putting it off. What obligates God to speak to us if He knows we aren't going to follow through and do what He says? Pride causes us to do that.

Obstacle #5: Lack of integrity

The fifth obstacle that hinders us from receiving the guidance of God is a *lack of integrity.* Proverbs 11:3 says, "The integrity of the upright will guide them, but the perversity of the unfaithful will destroy them."

Many dilemmas people face concerning the will of God boil down to issues of integrity: doing what is right and honest, for instance, or paying your brother what you owe him or not walking off a job without notice. Often the stalemate we encounter while making a decision is not so much a matter of wondering about God's direction as it is choosing whether or not to respond in integrity. If we understand biblical integrity, we won't need to ask God what to do nearly as often because we will already know what to do.

Let me describe what usually happens: A person at church borrows some money from another brother but fails to pay him back. After the relationship between the two is broken, the pastor intervenes to reconcile the problem. The ensuing conversation between the pastor and the offending person usually winds up like this:

"If you owe your brother, then you need to pay the debt."

"But I don't have that much."

"Then tell him what you *can* afford each month to pay it off."

"I'll do what I can."

Not long after that, the pastor discovers the guilty party didn't heed his advice and, curiously enough, "felt led" to attend another church. Eventually, the pastor hears through the grapevine the person's reason for leaving: "We used to attend Eagle's Nest, but now we feel the Lord is moving us on." God wasn't leading them to another church. God's will for that person's life was to take responsibility for himself and pay off his debts.

Now, if the pastor at the next church has any butter on his cracker, he'll call to find out why that family left this church. And if he discovers that they walked out defrauding a brother, he's a fool to receive them. But that's one of the ways countless people change churches year after year. It happens in charismatic and pentecostal churches as well as in other churches. Behavior such as this is not confined to one denomination or worship style.

Discovering the will of God often boils down to doing what's honest and upright. If walking in integrity means you're going to stir up a storm, don't worry. Let God defend you. But if you don't operate in integrity, He's under no obligation to fight for you. Dishonesty and a lack of integrity will only lead you out of the will of God and hinder your ability to be guided. So, if your decision comes down to a choice of walking in integrity or not, always choose integrity.

Obstacle #6:
Refusing to live an examined life

The sixth obstacle that will hinder us from discerning God's guidance is *refusing to live an examined life.* Proverbs 18:1 says, "A man who isolates himself seeks his own desire; he rages against all wise judgment."

People who refuse to examine their lives are defensive, they rarely apologize and they tend to isolate themselves from the input of others. They might be headed over a cliff, but they don't want to be told they're on the road to destruction. If they are Christians, their classic rationalization is, "I don't answer to man; I answer to God."

People who refuse to live an examined life arbitrarily choose from whom they will receive. Usually their list is pretty short, only including those who will say what they want to hear. Because the counsel they garner is one-sided, their decisions tend to go against all wise judgment.

Often a person's refusal to live an examined life is rooted in pride. We don't want to be told our faults, and we're offended if anyone else exposes them. Our pride insulates us from outside input and therefore from truth.

People who live an open, examined life, however, are lovers of truth. Take a look at what Paul wrote in his second letter to the Thessalonians:

> The coming of the lawless one is according to the working of Satan, with all power, signs, and lying wonders, and with all unrighteous deception among those who perish, because they did not receive the love of the truth, that they might be saved. And for this reason God will send them strong delusion, that they should believe the lie.
> —2 THESSALONIANS 2:9–11

Are you a lover of truth? Truth can hurt you, but it can also set you free. If you aren't a lover of truth, you won't listen to God's direction when you don't agree with Him.

In this passage God says to the people who are deceived by the spirit of antichrist, "Because you aren't a lover of truth, I will send you a lie, a delusion." The spirit of antichrist mentioned here deceives by telling people what they want to hear. But nonbelievers aren't the only ones who aren't lovers of truth; many Christians respond in the same way.

Truth must take priority over comfort. If I have treated a person wrongly, I'll go back and make it right because I love truth. Truth is the enemy of pride because pride compromises everything in the interest of self-preservation. Pride deludes us into believing we are the only ones who are right, that the problem is with the other person. The gate that opens us up to truth is our willingness to live an examined life.

If God said to me, "Godwin, you are cheap," I wouldn't like it. But if it were true, hearing the truth is only thing that would help me. If He said, "Rick, you are a liar," it would hurt. But if it were true, and I were to receive it and make the change, it would set me free.

Obstacle #7: Ignorance of God's Word

The seventh and final obstacle to tapping into God's guidance system is *ignorance of the Word of God*. In Psalm 119:105, God's Word is compared to a light: "Your word is a lamp to my feet and a light to my path."

The lamp of God's Word leads you only one step at a time on your journey. God doesn't give us a lamp that shines ahead of us from San Antonio to Oklahoma City; He gives us just enough to see our next step, and then the next step, and then the next. If we haven't obeyed the last step God has shown us, He won't give us more light! Because God wants us to be dependent on Him, in relationship with Him and close to Him, He gives us daily provision, step by step, a day at a time, until we arrive safely at our destinations. To do that, we have to know His Word.

But if I can't meet God in person—shake His

hand, see Him, feel Him or touch Him—how am I going to know what He's like? How am I going to know His heart? How am I going to know He's honest, righteous and just? How am I going to know how He thinks, how He feels and what He likes? Only through His Word can I know Him. God reveals Himself to us first in His Word. I can know everything *about* Him, but I cannot know *Him* apart from His Word.

If you have gone through a difficult situation in the past and face another formidable one in the future, how can you trust in a God you don't know? The only way we can know the God who leads us, the God who so earnestly pleads for us, is through His Word.

WHO'S YOUR BOSS?

So I ask you, who's your boss? If you haven't given the controls of your life to Jesus Christ, now is the time to make your life right with God. You don't have to get your life together first before giving it to Christ. No good deeds we do obligate Him to give us eternal life. The key to eternal life boils down to what we have done and what Christ has done.

What we have done: Every person has sinned and, as a result, is unable and unworthy to spend eternity with a perfect and sinless God. As a result, every person deserves eternity in hell—a place of torment, sorrow and hopelessness.

What Christ has done: Jesus died on the cross, a perfect Man who died for our sins and who offers every person forgiveness and eternal life. We receive forgiveness of sins and eternal life as we repent of our sins, acknowledging our need for the forgiveness Jesus gives and dedicating ourselves to live for Him.

If you have never done this, now is the perfect time. Pray this from your heart:

Dear Jesus, I acknowledge that I am full of sin and unable to save myself. I am sorry for my sins and I turn from them. I ask that You forgive me and cleanse me of all my sins. From this day forward I give the controls of my life to You as I commit myself to following You all the days of my life. Amen.

QUESTIONS FOR REFLECTION

1. Has pride ever hindered you from hearing from God? How?

_____

_____

_____

_____

_____

2. Read Matthew 21:28–32. Describe the self-deception of each of the two sons. Which one of the two sons are you more like? How can you avoid the errors of either son?

_____

_____

_____

_____

3. In which area of your life do you struggle with integrity? Why?

_____

_____

_____

_____

_____

4. Of the seven obstacles listed, which one did you relate to the most? Why does this obstacle have a grip on your life? What one thing can you do today to rid your life of one of these obstacles?

_____

_____

_____

_____

_____

Part II:

Cruising
Altitude

≈

3

Inner Conviction

AFTER VISITING FAMILY IN SAVANNAH, GEORGIA, A few years ago, my wife, Cindy, our baby daughter and I drove to the airport to board our eight-seater, twin engine Cessna 421 for a late evening flight home. Because the vertical stabilizer (the flap that runs up and down the tail) on that particular airplane is fairly big, a strong wind in a thunderstorm can bend it, even rip it, if it's not held securely in place when the airplane is grounded. I didn't want to run the risk of a strong wind damaging it, so earlier that day I placed a lock that somebody had just given me on the flap and then completely forgot about it.

When we arrived at the airport, it was eleven o'clock at night, and all I could think about was getting home. Because it was the first time I used the lock, it wasn't on my list of things to check before takeoff.

After completing the checklist we boarded the plane. I started the engines, closed the door, taxied down to the end of the runway and called the tower, "800MikeAlpha ready to take off." Radio control responded, "Cleared for takeoff; fly runway heading." I reached for the throttle, praying as I always did, "Lord, thank You for safety tonight on our flight home. In Jesus' name."

As I placed my hand on the throttle to begin our flight, instantly the term *rudder lock* flashed before my eyes—just as if the control tower had radioed the message to me. In the natural there was nothing in front of me to read. I certainly wasn't in a spiritual mood; it was eleven o'clock at night, and I was tired and ready to get home. But as I saw those words I froze and turned white as a sheet.

I'll never forget the feeling of my heart pounding and that gut-wrenching sigh as I realized how close to death we had come. Attempting to fly with a lock on the vertical stabilizer of an airplane is like driving your car without the use of the steering wheel. It isn't just a foolish mistake; it's a fatal mistake.

I called the tower, saying, "Hey, we need to shut the engines down for just a moment." After receiving their go-ahead, I got out of the plane and stared at the rudder lock still securely fastened to the vertical stabilizer. Another forty seconds into our journey and we would have crashed. The remains of my family would have been scattered along that Savannah runway.

There is no way I would have thought of that rudder lock on my own. It could only have been the inner conviction of the Holy Spirit leading me out of danger.

Have you ever been in a situation like this one in which you sensed something was wrong or something was about to happen? Have you ever had an unsettled feeling about a decision you have made? That's inner conviction, and the near-death experience I just described is an example of inner conviction at work. It operates like a sixth sense that enables God to guide us by the leading of His Holy Spirit.

This inner conviction is the first of the seven principles of God's guidance. Each principle is designed to keep you on course and headed in the right direction so you can avoid making any fatal errors.

As I mentioned in the introduction, the foundation in our study of God's guidance rests on Romans 8:14: "For as many as are led by the Spirit of God, these are sons of God." The sons of God—all believers in Jesus Christ—are *led* by the Spirit of God. If we belong to God, then God promises that He is *already* leading us. And if He is already leading us—or at least attempting to lead us—then it's best that we learn *how* He leads.

FIRST OBEDIENCE,
THEN FURTHER INSTRUCTION

In Acts 16, we find a great example of being led by the Spirit. Paul, Silas and Timothy were traveling, preaching the gospel. They made plans to head north into the interior of what is now Turkey. "After they had come to Mysia, they tried to go into Bithynia, *but the Spirit did not permit them*" (v. 7, emphasis added). Apparently, the Holy Spirit wouldn't allow them to travel into Asia; they knew that in their spirits. We read further:

> So passing by Mysia, they came down to Troas. And a vision appeared to Paul in the night. A man of Macedonia stood and pleaded with him, saying, "Come over to Macedonia and help us." Now after he had seen the vision, immediately we sought to go to Macedonia, concluding that the Lord had called us to preach the gospel to them.
>
> —ACTS 16:8–10

Notice that the Holy Spirit spoke to these men twice. The first time, they only had a partial understanding of what God had in store for them. How often does God give us direction, but He doesn't give us all the details? Only after they obeyed the first prompting of the Holy Spirit were they given further instructions.

But what would have happened had they

disobeyed, going on to Asia instead? It's a question we can't answer, but it's possible the Asian people wouldn't have been receptive to their message, perhaps even killing the greatest missionary in world history—Paul.

We find another example of this method of guidance in Acts 8. Philip, a deacon in the early church, was sent by an angel of God to walk down the road to Gaza. He had no idea why he was sent or where he was going; nevertheless, he obeyed. As he was walking, a chariot passed by carrying an Ethiopian eunuch, who happened to be reading from the Book of Isaiah. Once again, the Holy Spirit gave Philip further instructions after his initial act of obedience: "Then the Spirit said to Philip, 'Go near and overtake this chariot'" (v. 29).

So Philip ran to catch up with the chariot and asked the man reading the scroll, "Do you understand what you are reading?"

The man responded, "How can I, unless someone guides me?"

Philip explained the passage, which happened to be a messianic prophecy pertaining to Jesus, and led the eunuch to Christ. Then—coincidence of all coincidences—they encountered a pool of water on a desert road, so Philip baptized him.

God had that Ethiopian eunuch reading the right book, at the right place, at the right time, at the same moment the Holy Spirit impressed Philip to go join the chariot. Philip didn't know what was going to happen ahead of time, but after he obeyed, he saw a much clearer picture and a much higher purpose.

GOD STILL USES INNER CONVICTION

Stories about people's obedience to God's voice abound in Scripture. All too easily, however, we forget that God hasn't changed! Jesus is the same yesterday, today and forever. God still uses an inner conviction to guide us as we recognize and obey the promptings of the Holy Spirit.

An United 747 flight had just leveled off twenty minutes into its flight when cargo doors blew out, sucking passengers from their seats and out of the plane. The ensuing decompression in the cabin caused structural damage inside, injuring a number of the passengers and crew members—some severely.

What didn't get in the news was that just moments before the disaster, a Christian who was seated right where that accident was about to happen heard an inaudible voice saying, "Move to another area of the plane." He hesitated a moment, and it urged him again, "Move now." So he stood up and moved to an unoccupied seat in coach.

Moments later the cargo door blew open, causing extensive damage in the area where he had just been sitting. If he hadn't moved, he would have been severely injured and possibly killed. That's the ability to be led by an inner conviction.

Being led by the Holy Spirit isn't eerie or

mystical; it's simply the still, small voice of the Holy Spirit giving you a thought, a picture or an impression regarding the people and events around you. Sometimes He leads us without our realizing it—even when our hearts are hardened toward Him. God has equipped every believer with the potential to be led by the inner conviction of the Holy Spirit.

THE ANOINTING GUIDES US INTO ALL TRUTH

The apostle John wrote:

> But you have an anointing from the Holy One, and you know all things.... These things I have written to you concerning those who try to deceive you. But the anointing which you have received from Him abides in you, and you do not need that anyone teach you; but as the same anointing teaches you concerning all things, and is true, and is not a lie, and just as it has taught you, you will abide in Him.
>
> —1 JOHN 2:20, 26–27

In this passage John explained that believers, at salvation, are given an internal anointing of the Holy Spirit that seals them until the day of redemption—the day they will see Jesus face to face. This anointing operates apart from the infilling of the Holy Spirit and grants special access to the Father that nonbelievers do not have.

43

At salvation you have the capability of knowing all things. This anointing gives you the capacity for discovering truth but not necessarily from external sources. When John says, "You know all things," obviously he doesn't mean that all believers in Jesus Christ know everything. The anointing of the Holy Spirit, Jesus said in John 16:13, *guides us* into all truth.

Isn't it good to know that you can make the right decision, whether or not all the facts are at your disposal? Everything you need to know is available to you because God has anointed you with His Holy Spirit.

THE ANOINTING VALIDATES TRUTH

The anointing bears witness to what is truth and what isn't. When I hear truth from God's Word, it bears witness with the Spirit of truth inside of me. I can hear somebody sharing from God's Word, and inside, my spirit will say, "Yes, that's a word from God." Or, as I listen to someone, I may sense in my spirit that something is wrong with what that person is saying. I may not be able to pinpoint it, but I just have a check in my spirit that says, "No, that isn't a word from God."

Ultimately, then, the Holy Spirit acts as our Teacher, guiding us into all truth, even confirming or rejecting what we hear or read. He is the one who reveals anything that's knowable as He confirms things inside us apart from any outside sources.

A CAUTION ABOUT INNER CONVICTION

But here is the danger: The inner conviction is the most subjective of all the seven guiding principles because it is reliant solely upon what you feel, see and hear in your own spirit.

Some people make decisions, then hide behind the facade of inner conviction so they can be above reproach. People like this have come up to me and said, "The Lord told me that I am supposed to quit my job." When somebody says, "God told me," that indicates they have already taken me and everybody else out of the counseling process because they have already heard from the highest authority. What am I supposed to say? I'm not above God!

Do you know how I respond to that? I just say, "Well, God bless you." I never argue with them. They don't want my input; that's why they tell me, "God said." And because they took me out of the equation, I let them get what they wanted. And if I may say so, they deserve it. They didn't want truth, or they would have run through the checklist. People like that don't want to hear a *no;* they simply want to be told what they want to hear. And usually they can find someone who will comply. Louie Armstrong once said, "There are some people, if they don't know, you can't tell 'em!"

We need to be led by more than just inner conviction, because every Christian is a mixture of flesh and spirit. At salvation life is breathed into our dead spirits, giving us the right to our inheritance as sons of God so that we can be led by His Spirit. But we are still inextricably tied to our flesh, which not only guides us into sin but also inhibits us from clearly distinguishing God's guidance. So how can we tell the difference between what is rooted in the flesh and what is rooted in the spirit? We can identify lusts that are rooted in the flesh and avoid them.

THREE HINDERING MOTIVES

In 1 John 2 we are made aware of three areas of flesh weakness that can bring uncertainty to inner conviction: "Do not love the world or the things in the world. If anyone loves the world, the love of the Father is not in him. For all that is in the world—the *lust of the flesh,* the *lust of the eyes,* and the *pride of life*—is not of the Father but is of the world" (vv. 15–16, emphasis added).

All people gravitate toward three basic motives that foster fleshly rather than Spirit-led responses: The lust of the flesh craves *pleasure.* The lust of the eyes desires *possession.* The pride of life hungers for *position.* Because both fleshly and Spirit-led responses begin as motives, well-meaning Christians can easily confuse the flesh for the Spirit when applying the principle of inner conviction.

Since the beginning of time these three lusts have lured people away from making godly decisions. In the Garden of Eden God told Adam and Eve not to eat of the tree of the knowledge of good and evil. We learn in Genesis 3:6 that Eve saw that the tree was good for food—that's pleasure. She saw that it was pleasant to the eyes—that's possession. She saw that if she ate it, she would be like God—that's position.

Satan enticed Jesus with the same three temptations. After He was baptized by John the Baptist, Jesus was led by the Holy Spirit into the wilderness. At the end of His forty-day fast, the first voice He heard wasn't God's; it was the devil's. Knowing He was weakened by a forty-day fast, Satan tempted Jesus where He was most vulnerable. "You've gone a long time without food. You're weak and tired. If You were really the Son of God, You would turn these stones into bread."

Jesus knew Satan was tempting Him to use His divine power for His own pleasure. Now remember, feeding his lust for pleasure tripped up the first Adam and caused him to eat the fruit. But it didn't trip up the last Adam, Jesus. Rather than obey what His flesh told Him, Jesus replied, "Man shall not live by bread alone, but by every word that proceeds from the mouth of God" (Matt. 4:4).

Satan then challenged Him, "If You are the Son of God, jump off the temple, because God will send angels to protect You so You won't hurt yourself." In other words, "Jesus, jump off the temple to demonstrate Your position,

47

that You really are somebody."

But Jesus again refused, "It is written again, 'You shall not tempt the Lord your God'" (v. 7). Jesus didn't have to prove anything to anybody because He knew that His position came from who He was, not what He did.

Last of all, Satan tantalized Jesus with fleshly power. "All these kingdoms and their glory I will give You if You will worship me." Satan tempted Jesus with the best possessions this world has to offer.

But Jesus, refusing to compromise His purity and God's Word, responded, "Away with you, Satan! For it is written, 'You shall worship the LORD your God, and Him only you shall serve'" (v. 10).

After Jesus passed the test, He went out into His ministry and experienced the fruit that follows those who are led by the Spirit.

THREE QUESTIONS ABOUT MOTIVES

As you sense the inner conviction of the Holy Spirit urging you in a particular direction, ask yourself these three key questions:

- Does this fulfill fleshly pleasures?

- Do I think this will bring me security or esteem?

- Am I seeking to promote myself?

Let's examine these so we can recognize and eliminate them from the process of receiving God's guidance.

Question #1:
Does this fulfill fleshly pleasures?

Let me first say that God is not against pleasure. The psalmist wrote to God, "At Your right hand are pleasures forevermore" (Ps. 16:11). The pleasure that God is opposed to is the kind that feeds our fleshly lusts. Most people think that lust only involves sex, but that's just one type of lust. People seek pleasure through sex, money, work, addictions, even food—anything that feeds our selfish desires and operates as a substitute for an intimate relationship with God.

When you recognize that your inner conviction is pushing you to fulfill one of these selfish desires, remember that is not how God leads.

More importantly, God will never lead you to do something that violates His Word for the sake of selfish pleasures. He will never lead you to leave your spouse. He doesn't want you to change jobs if an increase in pay means it will cost you your integrity. God's desire is for us to look to Him first—not to worldy pleasures—to fill the hole in our hearts only He can fill.

Question #2: Do I think this will bring me security or esteem?

The lust for possessions is rooted in the desire to find security or esteem in the nicest house, the fanciest car or the fastest computer rather than in God. Unfortunately, people who seek security and esteem in things never find what they are looking for. They keep accumulating in order to fill that desire, but their actions become empty pursuits.

For the record, God is not against having possessions. The psalmist also wrote, "Let the LORD be magnified, who has pleasure in the prosperity of His servant" (Ps. 35:27). Repeatedly in Scripture we find that when God chose to bless someone, He blessed them with possessions. God blessed Abraham with great wealth. After Job went through his hardships, he acquired greater wealth than he had in the beginning.

But people lusting for possessions often sacrifice the present for the future in order to have what their lusts desire. They accumulate debt or neglect their families so they can experience the best life has to offer. They work overtime to keep up their house payments while neglecting the people who live inside. God is not opposed to parents providing for their families, but we shouldn't pursue pleasures at our family's expense, nor should we do so at the expense of our relationship with God. If you think God is leading you in this direction, think again.

Question #3:
Am I seeking to promote myself?

God isn't against position. "Therefore humble yourselves under the mighty hand of God, that He may exalt you in due time" (1 Pet. 5:6). The key lies in who is doing the promoting—you or God. God promises He will promote you in due time; the question is, Are you willing to wait for His perfect timing?

Many people hunger for the influence and respect that come with holding certain positions inside or outside the church. When a person gets angry because he isn't made an elder, when a person gets bitter and leaves the fellowship of other Christians because she hasn't been asked to sing on the worship team, that's lust for position. In fact, when a person gets upset because he or she hasn't been promoted soon enough, that's a sure sign that person isn't ready just yet.

When making decisions involving a change in position, it's important to ask yourself what your motivation is for making the change. Are you seeking the power to control people, or are you seeking to serve? Do you want to be in front of people because you like the prestige that goes with it, or because you sense God has called you to a more public ministry? Ask yourself these questions as you seek clarity on God's guidance.

LUSTFUL PURSUITS VS. BLESSINGS FROM GOD

When we make these three values—pleasure,

possession and position—our pursuit, they become lusts. When God bestows them freely upon us, within the guidelines of Scripture and in His timing, they become blessings. The key in all of this is, Who or what is our pursuit, and what is our motive?

The psalmist wrote, "Delight yourself also in the LORD, and He shall give you the desires of your heart" (Ps. 37:4). If I'm delighting in the Lord, my desire won't be to feed my flesh; it will be to please God. By making the delight of God my pursuit, I am giving Him room to bless me.

Jesus said, "If you abide in Me, and My words abide in you, you will ask what you desire, and it shall be done for you" (John 15:7). The more we abide in Christ—living, dwelling and staying continually in His presence—the greater the probability that our inner conviction will be right. The less we abide in the Lord, the more mixture there will be of flesh with the Spirit, and the more we will need other signs of confirmation. But when my heart is pure and I'm walking in that sweet intimate place with God, more times than not the inner conviction I sense will be from the Lord.

QUESTIONS FOR REFLECTION

1. Regarding the accounts of Paul, Silas and Timothy in Acts 16 and Philip in Acts 8, why do you think God waited for an initial act of obedience before giving further instruction? How does this principle apply to something that has happened to you this week?

_____

_____

_____

_____

2. Describe a time when you sensed God was leading you by the inner conviction of the Holy Spirit. How did He speak to you? Was it correct? If not, what do you think prevented you from sensing the inner conviction of the Holy Spirit accurately?

_____

_____

_____

_____

3. Read 1 Kings 19:9–18.

• What distractions did Elijah encounter?

_____

_____

• How would you expect God to speak to Elijah? How did God in fact speak to Elijah?

_____

_____

• How do you recognize that still, small voice in your life?

_____

_____

4. Take a moment to think of the roles of pleasure, possessions and position in your life. How does each get in the way of sensing God's inner conviction? What one thing can you do today to remove one of these lusts from your life?

_____

_____

4

Scriptural Confirmation

A GOOD PILOT HAS MASTERED HIS FLIGHT MANUAL. In fact, he knows it so well that he doesn't have to consult it every time he encounters turbulence. At times he may face decisions that the manual doesn't address, but because he understands the underlying principles contained in it, he knows what to do.

MASTERING GOD'S DIVINE FLIGHT MANUAL

The psalmist wrote, "Your word is a lamp to my feet and a light to my path" (Ps. 119:105). Like a training manual for pilots, God's inspired Word has been given to use for guidance and direction. Our effectiveness in navigating through seasons of difficult decision-making is contingent, to a great deal, upon the extent to which we know and apply the principles we have learned from our divine training manual, the Bible.

How often do we agonize over a decision, unaware that our solution lies in Scripture? Sometimes we don't even need to pray about the dilemma we face because God has already given us the answer in His Word.

Take, for example, a young Christian woman who falls in love with a man who is an unbeliever. Is it okay for a woman to marry a non-Christian? Despite her seemingly justifiable motives, if she has a working knowledge of the Word and a confidence in its trustworthiness, she would know that 2 Corinthians 6:14 instructs Christians not to be yoked together unequally with unbelievers. In the short run it may be painful breaking off a relationship with an unbeliever, but the dividends of obeying scriptural principles are eternal.

WHY WE NEED GOD'S WORD

Knowing the Word is crucial to godly decision-making because Scripture is God's primary means of speaking to us. The psalmist wrote, "Understanding your word brings light to the minds of ordinary people" (Ps. 119:130, CEV). A person doesn't need to be a Bible scholar or have a powerful prophetic ministry to hear from God. Any ordinary believer can receive direction from God when he or she has an understanding of God's Word. The more I eat the Word, meditate on it and apply it, the greater sense of God's direction I have.

People complain to me, "God doesn't tell me anything." But many of those people would hear from God if they would simply read their Bibles. Remember, the Spirit and the Word work together. God's Spirit—the Holy Spirit—speaks to us in the context of His Word. When we have the Word of God in us, the Holy Spirit has something with which to work.

When a business associate confides to you, "I think my fianceé is having an affair," what can you do or say to help him? If you have internalized the Word and made it a part of you, the Holy Spirit can bring scriptures to your remembrance at a time like this. When a mother confesses to you, "I'm losing control of my child," God is able to quicken to you what you have read in the Word. From that you can give wisdom, guidance, counsel and light.

GOD'S PATTERN FOR THE WORD AND THE SPIRIT

The Word of God is crucial in making sound decisions. But just as important is the work of the Holy Spirit to make God's Word real in our lives. Without the Holy Spirit to illuminate our spirits, the Word of God might seem like just another book of good principles. Without the Word of God, the Holy Spirit would lack the basis on which to speak into our lives. The two work together: The Spirit plays a part, but not without the Word. The Word plays a part, but not without the Spirit.

God follows this pattern when invading the

physical realm: He never acts apart from His Word and His Spirit, nor does He operate without bringing His Word and His Spirit together in agreement. By doing this, He demonstrates that His Spirit will never lead us in contradiction with His Word, and His Word will never lead us in contradiction with His Spirit. They always work in perfect harmony.

In Genesis 1 we read, "In the beginning God created the heavens and the earth. The earth was without form, and void; and darkness was on the face of the deep. And the Spirit of God was hovering over the face of the waters" (vv. 1–2). Notice that the Spirit of God—the Holy Spirit—was hovering, brooding over a created world without order. If God's desire is to invade it, how is He going to do it? Watch the pattern.

In verse 3 we read, "Then God said"—here comes the Word—"'Let there be light'; and there was light." See how the Spirit and the Word worked together to impact the physical realm?

Later we read, "Then God said"—here comes the Word again—"'Let Us make man in Our image, according to Our likeness...'" (v. 26). In Genesis 2, we see how God created Adam, "And the Lord God formed man of the dust of the ground, and *breathed* into his nostrils the breath of life; and man became a living being" (v. 7, emphasis added).

What's the breath of life? The Hebrew word for Spirit, *ruach,* is the same word for breath. The breath of life is the Spirit of God. God spoke the Word, "Let Us make man in Our image," then He formed the man out of the dust and breathed the Spirit of life into Adam.

So the Spirit and the Word always work in harmony and agreement with each other.

While working through decisions, Christians often follow one of two bits of guidance. The first says, "We just need to follow the leading of the Holy Spirit." The second says, "We just need to follow what the Word says." But God's response to us is, "Follow My Word *and* My Spirit, and make sure they are always in agreement."

THREE APPROACHES TO THE SPIRIT AND THE WORD

Most Christians approach the relationship between the Word of God and the Holy Spirit in the life of the believer in one of the following three ways:

All Spirit, no Word. Some believers have been endowed with a keen sensitivity to the workings of the Holy Spirit, but they have little or no knowledge of the Word. Occasionally their inclinations are correct, but because they are human, often their inclinations are wrong. Confusing the voice of their human spirit with the leading of the Holy Spirit, they are deceived. God warned through the prophet Ezekiel, "Woe to the foolish prophets, who follow their own spirit and have seen nothing" (Ezek. 13:3).

People like this are led to and fro by the

Spirit but rarely seem grounded in reality. The Spirit "leads" them to one church and then to another. God gives them a "word" for a young believer that may or may not apply to the person's situation. People who are all Spirit and no Word eventually self-destruct because they have no biblical parameters within which to work. When I describe people like this, I like to say, "No Word, all Spirit— you *blow up*." These people will always violate Scripture; they place feelings above clear Scripture.

All Word, no Spirit. Other believers have a hunger for the Word of God and an innate ability to master its content, but they have little or no sensitivity to the leading of the Holy Spirit.

People who are all Word and no Spirit are firmly grounded in reality—at times, a little too much so. They tend to doubt the supernatural and possess a pessimistic view of people. They pray for revival, but when it comes, they are the first ones to present all the "biblical" reasons why that particular move of God isn't a move of God at all. They pray for people in their community to be saved, but when discipling the new converts gets a little messy, they are the first to throw the book at any and all persons involved.

People who are all Spirit may at times seem nuts, but people who are all Word can be mean. Left to their compulsions, they become Pharisees—ministers of death rather than life. Paul wrote that the letter of the law kills, which is what these people are very adept at doing to believers and nonbelievers alike (2 Cor. 3:6).

Paul should know. When he was a Pharisee, he was given license to kill any follower of Jesus Christ. The Spirit, on the other hand, gives life (2 Cor. 3:6). But devoid of an openness to the life-giving Holy Spirit, the person who is all Word and no Spirit shrivels up and dies. When I describe people like this, I like to say, "All Word and no Spirit—you *dry up*."

Spirit and Word. When the Spirit and Word work in balance, people *grow up*. The operative word here is *balance*. The Spirit and the Word working together in harmony produce mature Christians whose lives emanate order and structure in cooperation with the free-flowing Spirit of God. God expects us to get in the Word *and* be led by the Spirit.

Above any of the other principles I share in this book, the Word and the Spirit in balance should always be your foremost guides. God will never lead you outside the boundary of His Word, and He will never guide you in disagreement with His Spirit. The two will always work together. You can count on it! Put it in the bank!

BALANCE IS BEST

Every believer, however, tends to lean toward the Spirit or the Word. Some people study better than they pray. Others pray better than they study. One isn't better than the other—we just need to work at keeping the two in balance.

Some people balance the two by minimizing the use of both. I guess you could refer to these people as "no Spirit, no Word" or "little Spirit, little Word." Believers who live like this can count on receiving from God about as much as they are willing to put in.

Everything we receive from God—including His direction—is a gift of God's grace, but without a knowledge of the Word or a sensitivity to the Spirit, He has little to work with in our lives. The key is being effective at knowing the Word of God and being led by the Spirit of God—and doing both in increasing measure.

BIBLICAL ILLITERACY: THE CHURCH'S NUMBER ONE PROBLEM

Success in obtaining direction from God increases with knowledge of the Word because the Holy Spirit then has more with which to work. The greater our knowledge of the Word, the fewer fatal mistakes we are likely to make.

According to the February 1997 issue of *Emerging Trends*, a publication of the Princeton Religion Research Center, "The churches of America face no greater challenge as we approach the next century than overcoming biblical illiteracy." The report goes on to say the American church faces a formidable challenge because many Americans don't know what they believe or why. Our faith is often rooted in our experience or upbringing rather than Scripture. We revere the Bible, but we don't read it; because we don't know the Bible, we find ourselves grasping for direction.

When we read the Word—eat it, chew on it, consume it and internalize it—we begin to see the big picture of how God acts, who He is, what He does and how He does it. As we examine the lives of men and women in the Bible, we learn the godly response to issues we face, decisions we make and directions we go. But if we don't know the Word of God, we're not going to make right choices.

FOUR KEYS TO READING GOD'S WORD FOR GUIDANCE

One of the reasons few believers look to God's Word for wisdom is that they don't know how to apply it to godly decision-making. Four keys enable us to better discern from the Bible God's direction for our lives: principles, patterns, people and prophetic parallels. Each key should be exercised prayerfully, ensuring that none of what is ascertained conflicts with Scripture.

Principles. When we search for guidance in the Word, we need to be looking for biblical principles. Reading for biblical principles begins by searching out *explicit* direction in Scripture regarding a given decision. A great deal of the stress we feel when making a decision would be relieved if we only knew what Scripture explicitly said and trusted it enough to follow through.

63

For example, we don't need to wonder whether or not to financially support our local church or the ministries through which we're being fed spiritually. Jesus told His disciples to accept what people provided for them because "the laborer is worthy of his wages" (Luke 10:7).

We also know from the Bible that priests in the Old Testament received offerings from those they served. This biblical principle is found throughout the Word of God, so we can trust it without needing to receive a special word from God regarding it.

Because the Bible was written in a culture and time period much different from ours, the underlying principles that apply to us may not be readily seen. But the principles that applied in situations two thousand years ago have a crossover effect today. This is called implicit direction.

Paul addresses issues regarding eating meat sacrificed to idols in 1 Corinthians 8. This may seem totally irrelevant in our culture— one that has no place for idol worship and temple restaurants. However, we can find the implicit or underlying principle of this passage: The freedom we have in our own decision-making that results from our spiritual maturity should never cause young believers to stumble.

We should always look for the underlying principle and not get distracted by the cultural differences.

Patterns. A Bible story or passage by itself may offer a variety of applicable biblical principles. When these principles are compared to similar circumstances elsewhere in Scripture, biblical patterns emerge.

As the Old Testament progresses, a pattern appears involving Israel's relationship with God: First Israel worships God in unhindered fellowship, then they fall away from God and experience hardship and suffering. After crying out for forgiveness, they are restored back to fellowship with Him. Despite being restored, God's chosen people fall away again. After a time of suffering, they repent and are forgiven once more. (See 1 and 2 Chronicles.)

So we see a pattern of God forgiving His people over and over when they come to Him with hearts of true repentance. We learn from this particular pattern that God will receive us when we come to Him truly repentant—despite the number of times we have fallen away.

People. Studying the lives of men and women in the Bible can provide some of the most practical lessons in God's guidance. To those who are shrewd enough to learn from the successes and failures of others, God's Word offers a vast storehouse of resources. Lessons we learn from the lives of others can save us from making faulty decisions ourselves.

From David we see how to respond to hardship; from Saul we learn how *not* to respond to hardship. Abraham teaches us that even when we take great risks, if we are led by the Spirit, God will take care of us.

From Joseph we discover that sharing a big dream with small-thinking people may get us in trouble. Sharing dreams with brothers in the same business may even incite them to jealousy and abuse. Joseph's story also shows us that sometimes when we do right, yet wrong things happen, God may be taking us on a sovereign detour. Because Joseph was faithful to God in the face of suffering and injustice, he experienced great blessing and was promoted above every person in Egypt except Pharaoh himself.

The life of Job shows us that being right and being righteous will not prevent us from being attacked. But also from Job we realize that hardship only lasts a season. If we refuse to deny our faith in God, whatever has been stolen can be restored to us in greater quantity, quality or kind. Because of this we should never forfeit hope in God just to wallow in self-pity and become mean, defeated or bitter.

Prophetic parallels. John grew up in a small, midwestern town, appreciating the security and safety rural areas provide. But as he grew in the faith, he sensed a desire to reach the masses for Christ. During his times of prayer the Holy Spirit urged him to pray about planting a church in Chicago. Knowing that a burden is not necessarily a release, he waited for God to give him the go-ahead.

"Lord," he prayed, "although I know You love the people I've grown up with, I also feel You've given me a burden to reach more than just the thousand people who live in this town. If You want me to plant a church in Chicago, I'm going to need specific direction from You and a sign that You are in this."

One morning while reading his Bible, he stumbled across Psalm 107:6–7: "Then they cried out to the LORD in their trouble, and he delivered them from their distress. He led them by a straight way to a city where they could settle" (NIV). He paused to read the last phrase again, "He led them by a straight way to a city where they could settle."

As he prayed, the Holy Spirit revealed to him, "Today is the day I am opening the door for you to move to the city." Later that day, he was offered a job in Chicago that would provide his means of support while planting a church. God used the Scriptures to provide a prophetic parallel into John's life.

At times while you're reading the Bible, God may bring to the surface His direction, which may be totally unrelated to the context of the passage. Reading for a prophetic parallel requires a keen sensitivity to the Holy Spirit and feet planted firmly in the knowledge of Scripture. This operates most effectively as a means of confirmation and will never contradict Scripture or violate the witness of the Spirit inside you. Notice that John didn't rely on the prophetic parallel as his primary means for direction. He already had the inner conviction, and his desire was scriptural; God also provided the right circumstances and the provision.

Some people use this method as a means

of coercing God to justify what they are going to do anyway. People like this close their eyes, open their Bible and use whatever scripture their fingers point to as guidance. That is simply immaturity mixed with misunderstanding.

Using prophetic parallels as the primary means of discerning God's will is fraught with pitfalls. As I continue to say throughout this book, when making a decision, a person needs multiple witnesses—with this being only one. In the right circumstances and when confirmed by the inner conviction of the Holy Spirit, God can use a prophetic parallel in Scripture to give you specific direction.

GOD'S WORD BRINGS SUCCESS

God spoke to the Israelites as they were about to cross the Jordan into the Promised Land:

> This Book of the Law shall not depart from your mouth, but you shall meditate in it day and night, that you may observe to do according to all that is written in it. For then you will make your way prosperous, and then you will have good success.
> —JOSHUA 1:8

Notice the passage says, "Then *you* will make your way prosperous." God says that if you meditate on His Word and obey it, you will have good success. That doesn't mean you'll never encounter any problems or obstacles; it means that when all is said and done, you'll find success. That's a promise.

Put the Word on tape, write it down, read it, listen to it, get it inside you; then you'll find the Word working in your life. Difficult decisions will get easier. As God gives you the courage to obey it, you'll discover over time the success God's Word brings.

Questions for Reflection

1. Have you ever received scriptural confirmation about something into which you felt God was guiding you? What happened?

_____

_____

_____

2. Do you enjoy God's Word? Why or why not?

_____

_____

_____

3. What one thing is keeping you from spending more time in God's Word? What can you do to change that today?

_____

_____

_____

4. What decision are you facing now on which you could use God's guidance? Stop and ask the Lord now to guide you by His Word.

_____

_____

_____

5

Prophetic
Corroboration

THE COPILOT OF AN AIRCRAFT PLAYS A CRUCIAL role. Not only does the copilot perform certain tasks on the airplane, but he or she also serves in relief of the pilot. The copilot affirms the direction the pilot is headed. Should the pilot head in the wrong direction, the copilot is there to re-direct him. The copilot doesn't guide the plane, but enhances what the pilot is already doing.

In the same way, God gives us prophetic *corroboration* as a means of discerning His will. According to the *American Heritage Dictionary*, to *corroborate* means "to strengthen or support with other evidence." Prophecy corroborates the work that God is already doing in our lives. It most often plays a supportive role.

In this chapter we will look at the role

prophecy plays in discovering God's direction. Although the most neglected among the seven principles of God's guidance, prophecy can be extremely helpful when exercised with discernment and measured against the Word of God.

THE VALIDITY OF PROPHECY

Some believe prophecy died with the New Testament apostles, but Scripture clearly does not support this belief.

The prophet Joel foretold of the day when men and women would prophesy:

> And it shall come to pass afterward that I will pour out My Spirit on all flesh; your sons and your daughters shall prophesy, your old men shall dream dreams, your young men shall see visions.
> —JOEL 2:28

Before Pentecost only a select group of people—mostly men—maintained a divine link to God. People relied on prophets and priests who heard God's voice and spoke on His behalf. But when the Spirit of God was poured out on all believers at Pentecost, the apostle Peter declared Joel's prophecy fulfilled (Acts 2:14–21). As a result of Pentecost, all believers—men and women alike—can receive from God the ability to hear His voice and, to varying degrees, to prophesy. Even though all may prophesy, not all are prophets. Not everyone will serve in the office of a prophet, but every believer has been gifted to hear the Spirit's voice and share it with other people.

So, prophecy was valid during the time of the apostles, but what about today? The writer of Hebrews wrote, "Jesus Christ is the same yesterday, today, and forever" (13:8). One of the core doctrines of our faith states that God is changeless. That doesn't refer only to the Father, but also to the Son and the Holy Spirit. We can change God's mind through prayer, but His character and His ways are changeless.

Some well-meaning Christians perform theological gymnastics in order to prove that prophecy is no longer valid. In no place in Scripture are we explicitly told that God would stop pouring out His Spirit before we see Him face to face. Prophecy, tongues, healing, miracles—the whole package—are just as available today as they were two thousand years ago. The problem is, abuses of prophecy as well as fear have caused the church to minimize prophecy's role or to doubt its existence altogether.

THE PURPOSE OF PROPHECY

In 1 Corinthians 14 Paul gave very clear instructions on governing prophecy in the church. To begin, he explained prophecy's purpose: "But he who prophesies speaks *edification*

75

and *exhortation* and *comfort* to men" (v. 3, emphasis added). Let's look at each of these.

Edification. The Greek word for *edify, oiko-domeo,* literally means "to build a house." People used this word when referring to building a home, but it was also applied to the building up of godly character and integrity in the believer or in a body of believers. A prophetic word, aptly spoken, will build up and not tear down the believer. A true prophetic word compels us toward a closer walk with God and builds us up in our faith.

Exhortation. According to Vine's Expository Dictionary, the Greek word for *exhort, para-kaleo,* means "to admonish, exhort, to urge one to pursue some course of conduct." Exhortation stirs us to obey God's will, moving us from thought to action. Often, the New Testament writers used this word when referring to the Holy Spirit, the Exhorter. Although the Holy Spirit can be described as the Comforter, God knows better than to allow us to remain in the safety of our comfort zones. He spurs us on toward love and good works.

Comfort. Both exhortation and comfort give the sense of encouragement. While exhortation looks to future conduct, comfort deals with a trial experienced in the present or past. According to Vine's, the Greek word for *comfort, paramuthia,* literally means "near speech," which communicates a greater degree of tenderness than exhortation. When you have experienced a trial or difficult situation, you need a tender word from the Holy Spirit through prophecy to encourage and comfort you.

Prophecy, then, builds up our godly character, sends us out to do God's will and cheers us up when we are discouraged.

PROPHECY BENEFITS THE CHURCH

Paul continues, "He who speaks in a tongue edifies himself, but he who prophesies edifies the church" (v. 4). The purpose of prophecy is the edification of the whole church, not just the individual. God doesn't give you a gift so you can have your spiritual buzz and feel good.

Everything God does is redemptive. He doesn't destroy, tear down or divide; He builds up. He desires to strengthen His body. Even when He takes us to the woodshed, He does it to redeem His purpose in us, not to drive us away or hurt us. He corrects us so we can fulfill the good purposes He has for our lives. A prophetic word can have a minor rebuke, but it will never demean or pronounce, "You are the devil." It may encourage you to endure or to cleanse yourself from sin, but it will edify you, it will exhort you and it will comfort you.

FORTH-TELLING AND FORETELLING

Most biblical scholars, whether or not they

believe in the validity of contemporary prophecy, would define prophecy as a combination of "forth-telling" and "foretelling." Forth-telling speaks a word from God concerning present circumstances, while foretelling reveals future events. In either case, the word spoken is a divine enablement—no person conjures up their own word from God. The Book of Revelation gives us prime examples of both.

In the first three chapters of Revelation Jesus "spoke forth" to the seven churches in Asia, addressing their behavior and spiritual condition, hence the word *forth-telling*. Forth-telling reveals the current attitudes of the heart.

The next nineteen chapters in Revelation "foretell" future events regarding the last days and judgment. Many of these prophecies have yet to be fulfilled; they foretell events that haven't occurred yet. Both Old Testament and New Testament prophecies operated in one or both aspects of forth-telling and foretelling. The same can be said of contemporary prophecy.

FIVE TYPES OF PROPHECY

Scripture gives us five different ways God uses the foretelling and forth-telling elements of prophecy to direct and instruct. Let's examine each one.

Conferral prophecy. Paul writes to Timothy, "Do not neglect the gift that is in you, which was given to you by prophecy with the laying on of the hands of the eldership" (1 Tim. 4:14). This shows us that a gifting can be conferred on a person by the Holy Spirit through the laying on of hands and prophecy.

Correctional prophecy. God directs and instructs using this method. In the Book of Amos God speaks through the prophet Amos to chastise Israel for favoring the wealthy and taking advantage of the poor. He corrects them through the use of prophecy.

Judgment prophecy. Although rare, prophecies speaking of impending judgment are biblical. In Acts 5 the apostle Peter pronounced to Ananias and Sapphira individually that they were each going to die because they lied to God. And they fell down dead—immediately. Peter pronounced God's judgment on this husband and wife for lying to the Holy Spirit.

Directional prophecy. This type of prophecy is also rare. In 1 Samuel 10 Samuel instructed Saul where to go in order to find his lost donkeys. Samuel knew this through God and prophesied it to Saul. This was prophecy that gave directions. Directional prophecy isn't very common in the New Testament, so it must be treated with a great deal of caution and discernment.

Confirmational prophecy. This is the most common form prophecy takes. On one of his missionary trips Paul was prompted by the Holy Spirit to return to Jerusalem, where he would be imprisoned and turned over to the Romans. While on his return, he was

79

given a number of prophecies confirming his impending imprisonment. Paul confirms this to the elders of the church at Ephesus: "And see, now I go bound in the spirit to Jerusalem, not knowing the things that will happen to me there, except that the Holy Spirit testifies in every city, saying that chains and tribulations await me" (Acts 20:22–23).

The inner conviction of the Holy Spirit *bound* Paul to return to Jerusalem. He was probably bound by the Holy Spirit because if he had been allowed to have his own way, he wouldn't have gone. What was ahead for him wasn't easy, so the Holy Spirit confirmed to Paul along the way what was going to happen in order to prepare him.

During a meeting with a group of believers in Caesarea, Agabus, a prophet, took Paul's belt, tied up his own hands and feet and prophesied that the owner of the belt would be bound and delivered into the hands of the Gentiles (Acts 21:10–11). What Agabus spoke didn't change what was going to happen nor did his prophecy give any specific direction, but it did confirm to Paul what God had previously spoken to him. Confirmational prophecy confirms the inner conviction of the Holy Spirit.

Almost all true prophecy is confirmational. Ninety percent of the prophecies given in my church from experienced prophets such as Bill Hamon, Kim Clement and Mark Chironna have been confirmational. They aren't telling us anything new; they're confirming our potential. Even if what they're prophesying isn't happening just yet, the prophecy confirms what God intends to do in us and what He *is* doing in us. People who are in relationship with the person being prophesied over recognize what the prophecy is confirming. So many times, my heart has been warmed just to have God's work in me confirmed by somebody who knows nothing about me.

SAFEGUARDS AGAINST THE MISUSE OF PROPHECY

Prophecy is dangerous when unchecked, but when certain safeguards are in place it is a valid means of confirmation.

Not long ago the headlines were rife with stories surrounding the Heaven's Gate cult. Thirty-nine Nike-wearing computer jocks "shed their containers" one March day in 1997 as they awaited a rendezvous with their alien masters behind the Hale-Bopp comet. One of the two prophets who led his followers into the mass suicide was, in fact, the son of a Presbyterian minister. Fears of a Heaven's Gate repeat performance cause people to avoid prophets and prophecy altogether.

Prophecy is like gasoline. When channeled correctly, it is powerful; when misused or abused, it is explosive and devastating. Whether in a worship service or a personal encounter, two safeguards can prevent the misuse and abuse of this gift.

Safeguard #1:
Know the person's character.

The first safeguard to directional and confirmational prophecy is knowing the character of the person behind the word. Paul wrote to the Thessalonians, "And we urge you, brethren, to recognize those who labor among you" (1 Thess. 5:12). *Recognize* literally means "to know"—not in an intimate sense, but in a general sense of having an understanding into a person's nature or character.

If someone appears in your fellowship out of nowhere and starts giving prophetic words to everyone, what is your assurance that this person is of trustworthy character? I wouldn't want a dishonest person or someone with sinful or destructive habits prophesying over me or anybody else in my congregation.

Whether you receive a prophecy in a worship service or on the phone, make sure that the person giving the word is submissive to *your* church's leadership and under the covering of a local fellowship. Anyone who says, "I don't answer to man; I answer to God," is a disaster waiting to happen. Plenty of people have succeeded in using prophecy as an illegitimate means of garnering power and control. My book *Exposing Witchcraft in the Church* specifically addresses the problem of rebellion and control in the local congregation.

Safeguard #2:
Judge the word.

Paul writes to the Corinthians, "Let two or three prophets speak, and let the others judge" (1 Cor. 14:29). Here we see liberty and limitation. Prophets were given the liberty to speak, but there was a limitation of the number of prophecies to be given and on how the words were to be received.

All prophecy must be judged, because no person is above the Word of God. It doesn't matter how many books a person has written or whether or not he has a television show. If the last ninety-nine prophetic words the person gave were on the money, the next prophetic word must be judged.

In the Old Testament if a prophecy was wrong or it wasn't fulfilled, the prophet was stoned. That would ruin the lives of some contemporary prophets, wouldn't it? Because Jesus has fulfilled the Law, we no longer judge the prophet; we judge the word he or she gives. And we judge that word against God's Word.

One evening Darla marched through the front door and announced to Tim, "Because you have been negligent as the spiritual authority in our house, God is releasing me from our wedding vows."

Although he attended church semiregularly, Tim never seemed to find much interest in spiritual things. After a job injury forced him onto disability, the added pressure served to drive a deeper wedge between him and Darla.

As Tim increasingly isolated himself due to his depression, Darla immersed herself in a women's prayer group.

Darla enjoyed the relationships that developed there and was particularly impressed with another woman in the group. Although still very embittered by her own failed marriage, Kathy generated a commanding presence. Her prayers seemed to penetrate the inner sanctum of God, and her knowledge of Scripture was unparalleled. Most of all, she was gifted in prophecy.

One evening during a prayer meeting, Kathy spoke to Darla, "I sense God is saying to you that He is closing certain doors and opening new ones. God says to you, 'Because you have endured spiritual unfaithfulness in your house, I am now releasing you from the unfaithful one.'" That was all the evidence Darla needed.

But was that prophetic word faithful and sure? Should Darla just act on it, or judge it against the Bible as well?

God's Word says, "And a woman who has a husband who does not believe, if he is willing to live with her, let her not divorce him" (1 Cor. 7:13). Prophecy always bows down to Scripture. It will never contradict, supersede or replace it.

Prophecy can be dangerous when used as the sole means of decision-making. The principle overriding all seven principles of guidance is that two or three principles at a minimum need to agree to confirm your decision. Obviously, the more important the decision or the greater the risk, the more confirmation you need.

NO ONE IS PERFECT

Even the godliest person can be off. When you were younger, do you remember drinking water out of the garden hose on a hot day? What did it taste like? It tasted like rubber because the water came through the rubber hose. Any prophetic word given by a human being will be tainted by human nature.

If a prophet is intimidated by having his word judged, then he is immature and in error. No one should take it personally, because no one is right every time. The most assuring words you can hear from someone who gives you a prophetic word are, "Make sure and test it."

When someone comes to you with a word from God, have the person write their prophecy down. If *you* write it down, you may add to the word. If you commit the word to memory, you'll either forget the gist or you'll change it. It's amazing how people over time can misconstrue what someone has told them—usually it ends up taking shape according to what the beneficiary of the prophecy wanted it to be.

Judge the prophecy with the Word of God, but also test it with the other principles of God's guidance system. Does the inner conviction of your spirit give witness to the word that was given? Is it supported by godly counsel? Do the principles of provision, peace and circumstantial evidence back it up? If the prophetic word does not pass the test, you're a fool to follow it.

PROPHETIC CORROBORATION BRINGS PEACE

Paul tells us, "For God is not the author of confusion but of peace" (1 Cor. 14:33). Although I will discuss this principle of inner peace in greater detail later, let me say that the peace of God must be the fruit of a prophetic word. If the product of a prophetic word is confusion, guess what isn't there? Peace. "And let the peace of God rule in your hearts" (Col. 3:15). If you sense more confusion than peace, the Holy Spirit probably isn't behind that word of prophecy.

Paul continues, "Therefore, brethren, desire earnestly to prophesy, and do not forbid to speak with tongues" (1 Cor. 14:39). Despite the risks and potential hazards involved, we still should aspire to prophesy. Paul says to "desire *earnestly* to prophesy." When prophecy is off, it's really off. But when prophecy speaks the heart and destiny of God, it breathes life into an otherwise barren existence.

AN OX OR A CLEAN STALL?

Doing the will of God always involves an element of risk because God loves faith. Proverbs 14:4 says, "Where no oxen are, the crib is clean: but much increase is by the strength

86

of the ox" (KJV). A crib in Old Testament times was either a manger or a stall for holding cattle. Taking care of livestock is messy business, but there is one way you can ensure that the stall will be kept clean—by keeping no cattle at all.

Living by the Spirit of God works in the same way. Most of the people I grew up with in the ministry wanted a clean stall. Avoiding the potential for any hint of a mess, they were content to minister without the power of the Holy Spirit. They merely dealt in the intellectual transmittal of information. The stall was clean, but they had no life.

But by buying an oxen, you assure yourself of a mess. You also increase your chances of making a profit. With the risk comes the increase. If I had to choose between a harvest and a clean stall, I would choose the harvest every time.

QUESTIONS FOR REFLECTION

1. Has prophecy ever played a role in your life? Was it positive or negative? If you had a negative experience, what do you think went wrong (based on what you just learned about prophecy)?

_____

_____

_____

_____

2. How important is judging a word of prophecy? Do you have any hesitations in judging prophecy? If so, examine them now. Where did they originate? How can you release them to God right now?

_____

_____

_____

_____

3. Are you open to receiving prophecy? Why
   or why not? Are you open to prophesying?
   Why or why not?

_____

_____

_____

_____

_____

4. If you had the choice of the harvest or a
   clean stall, which would you really choose?
   Why? Do you believe this is God's choice
   for you?

_____

_____

_____

_____

_____

6

Godly Counsel

ALTHOUGH EVERY VOCATION CARRIES WITH IT A degree of stress, statistical studies consistently indicate that working in air traffic control is one of the most stressful jobs in the workplace. Why? Pilots may have the lives of a few hundred people in their care, but air traffic controllers must coordinate the flight patterns of numerous airplanes in order to prevent midair collisions. One error can result in the loss of many hundreds of human lives.

Air traffic controllers observe by radar what the pilot in the airplane is unable to see. Godly counsel operates much the same. People consult godly men and women in order to gain a perspective they don't have.

Air traffic controllers give directives, yet they are powerless to make a pilot obey.

Neither are people bound to obey the advice of godly counsel. But good pilots refuse to stray from air traffic control's recommendations—even when they contradict what they can or cannot see. People who walk in a submitted relationship to godly counsel know better than to veer too far from the guidance of people they respect.

Ted worked with a parachurch organization in a college town. Known for his "in-your-face" style, Ted built a college discipleship ministry from nothing into one of the most influential student organizations on campus. His charismatic, risk-taking personality endeared him to both the students and his financial supporters. Ted would try just about anything once if it would win an audience on campus.

People also knew that the dark side of Ted's personality—his bullheadedness—was part of the package when dealing with Ted. When he got an idea, there was no changing his mind. Ted focused that same aggressive energy on maintaining an active financial support base.

When Phil, who was discipled under Ted's ministry while in college, approached Ted about a way to raise a large amount of money fairly quickly for his ministry, Ted saw this as a golden opportunity. All his supporters needed to do was to deposit a sum of their own money in a specific charitable foundation for six months. Then the money would be returned to the investors, with the same amount being donated by the foundation to Ted's college ministry. Phil explained all the details to Ted. They involved charitable excess funds, earnest money and Phil as a go-between. It sounded great.

"I don't get a good feeling about this," Ted's area supervisor cautioned him. "I just don't understand why your supporters need to give earnest money just to prove you have financial support."

"I would think the same thing," Ted countered, "except that I've known Phil since he was a student. He's a Christian and an extremely successful businessman. I discipled him myself. Besides, the proceeds aren't going directly into my pocket—they're going to benefit our ministry here at school. Now we can afford to purchase a van, a new computer and the office furniture we need so badly."

Despite the reservations voiced by a minority of the people Ted respected, he approached the new fund-raising idea wholeheartedly as he did everything else. In no time, the funds were raised and deposited in Phil's charitable organization.

Within two months area newspapers were full of stories alleging a Ponzi scheme (a swindle that promises a quick return) under Phil's direction. Because Ted had encouraged his supporters to invest money in this organization, he found himself at the center of the controversy. Within three months Ted knew that neither he nor his supporters would ever see their money again.

Had Ted listened to godly counsel, he would have saved himself both stress and heartache. In the end, Ted not only lost multiple thousands of dollars, but he also lost the trust of people who looked up to him.

COUNSELING IS SECOND NATURE TO GOD

One of the most amazing facets of God's love is that He trusts us. Despite His omnipotent power to intervene in our lives, He entrusts to us the decisions we make along with the consequences that accompany them. But God doesn't abandon us to our shortcomings and weaknesses. He also reveals us to the side of His character that gives us guidance and counsel.

Seven hundred years before Jesus' birth the prophet Isaiah used these words to describe the coming Messiah:

> For unto us a Child is born, unto us a Son is given, and the government will be upon His shoulder. And His name will be called Wonderful, *Counselor*, Mighty God, Everlasting Father, Prince of Peace.
> —ISAIAH 9:6, EMPHASIS ADDED

Did you notice that Jesus is described as the Counselor? In Jesus, the Son of God, we have one who is not only all-wise, but one who freely shares His wisdom with people. The very nature of Jesus is to give His followers counsel!

So how does Jesus give us counsel? He

shares His infinite wisdom with us through the Holy Spirit. Isaiah later describes the Spirit through whom the Messiah would eventually minister:

> There shall come forth a Rod from the stem of Jesse, and a Branch shall grow out of his roots. The Spirit of the LORD shall rest upon Him, the Spirit of wisdom and understanding, *the Spirit of counsel* and might, the Spirit of knowledge and of the fear of the LORD.
> —ISAIAH 11:1–2, EMPHASIS ADDED

Jesus' ministry on earth was empowered through seven manifestations of the Holy Spirit, one of which was the Spirit of counsel. If Jesus ascended to heaven, leaving His Spirit to empower believers, then that same Spirit of counsel is at work in the body of Christ today. Godly, life-giving counsel is a sign of the Holy Spirit at work among His people.

THE BENEFITS OF GODLY COUNSEL

God never intended for Christians to be isolated from other believers. It's easier to venture out on our own, but Scripture promises benefits to those who seek godly counsel:

> Where there is no counsel, the people fall; but in the multitude of counselors there is safety.
> —PROVERBS 11:14

95

Safety. Without counsel, people make decisions at their own peril. But when a multitude of counselors are involved, the outcome is safety. Notice that the context of this passage points to *multiple* counselors. There's safety in numbers. The more people you consult, the less chance there is of getting faulty counsel.

Any person facing a life-or-death decision concerning a medical condition would be foolish not to secure multiple opinions from a variety of doctors. If we do that for an organ, why wouldn't we be even more concerned about our future, our purpose and the will of God in our lives? I can get by without a toe, but I can't get by apart from the will of God if I'm going to fulfill my destiny and purpose.

A multitude of counselors functions like a lifeboat. If you were on a ship that began to sink in the middle of a storm, would you prefer to bob up and down in a lifeboat by yourself, or would you prefer to tie your lifeboat to other lifeboats? The answer is obvious. Multiple lifeboats attached to one another won't overturn or sink nearly as easily as a single lifeboat will.

> Plans fail for lack of counsel, but with many advisers they succeed.
> —PROVERBS 15:22, NIV

Success. Many advisors not only provide safety, but they also ensure success. If you are considering a decision, but you refuse to take it to godly counsel because "they wouldn't understand," you stand a good chance of missing out on the success God has for you. No matter how intelligent you are, it is physically and intellectually impossible to develop and explore every option. Sometimes even a slight adjustment based on advice from an objective third party makes the difference between success and failure.

Following the counsel of one person is risky. However, if you consult many counselors for advice regarding the same problem, each one will offer different insight into your situation. Rarely will one individual give you all the insight you are in search of, but when brought together with the insight of other counselors we often find clearer direction.

> By pride comes nothing but strife, but with the well-advised is wisdom.
> —PROVERBS 13:10

Averting future conflict. An associate pastor departs a church in anger because the leadership didn't see things his way. He decides the solution to the problem is to plant a church that siphons members from his former church. As a result, the new church he plants becomes a source of conflict between the people who choose to stay and the people who choose to follow the associate pastor. In the process, lives are hurt; some people caught in the cross fire stop attending church altogether.

Had the young man humbled himself, submitted to godly leadership and sought counsel, he may have been convinced to reconcile rather than divide the body of Christ.

At the root of conflict you will always find pride. Before making decisions based on pride, we're better off seeking the advice of level-headed men and women who can offer a different perspective. Seeking counsel requires humility. Sometimes we're so filled with pride that we would rather fail or stir up trouble than seek counsel from someone who "might not understand."

> The way of a fool is right in his own eyes, but he who heeds counsel is wise.
> —PROVERBS 12:15

Revealing blind spots. Have you ever eaten at a restaurant, only to discover after arriving home and looking in the mirror that you spent the whole evening with a chive lodged between your front teeth? Then it dawned on you why your friends laughed so hysterically at your jokes! Then you kick yourself, saying, "Why didn't my friends tell me I had that chive stuck between my teeth? They could have at least sent me to the bathroom so I could see myself in the mirror!"

The problem is, God did not create you with the ability to see your teeth; they happen to lie in your blind spot. We all need other people to give us God's perspective because it is impossible for any one of us to see the whole picture. Godly counsel is the mirror that enables us to identify our blind spots. You're a fool to go your own way when godly counsel is available. The fool will do what's right in his own eyes; however, if you want to be wise, seek godly counsel.

> Therefore thus says the Lord GOD: "Behold, I lay in Zion a stone for a foundation, a tried stone, a precious cornerstone, a sure foundation; *whoever believes will not act hastily.*"
> —ISAIAH 28:16, EMPHASIS ADDED

Waiting on God. Recently, I was with Ralph Mahoney of World Map, a man I admire very much, and he made this comment: "Any time there is a hurry-up feeling in your spirit— pressure—and you can't wait for godly counsel, you will crash." If you're about to make a decision on marriage, business, borrowing money or buying that new car, and you're in a hurry, under pressure to decide right now—don't you dare move.

God will never put you in the position where you have to make a crucial decision without counsel. If it fits into God's plan for your life, you will have the time to secure godly advice. That may take a day or two. The bigger the decision, the more time you need to take to secure godly counsel.

99

The New Revised Standard Version interprets the last phrase of Isaiah 28:16 this way: "One who trusts will not panic." Panic and trust work in opposite directions. If we truly trust God, we will refuse to panic and make hasty decisions.

Jesus was never in a hurry. When Mary and Martha sent word to Jesus that His good friend Lazarus was sick, He didn't immediately jump onto His donkey. By the time He arrived in Bethany, Lazarus had been dead for four days. Mary even confronted Jesus about His tardiness: "Lord, if You had been here, my brother would not have died" (John 11:32). In Mary and Martha's opinion, Jesus was late.

Sometimes, by slowing down the decision-making process, we may appear to pass up what seems to be once-in-a-lifetime opportunities. Taking the time to secure godly counsel might mean forfeiting the very opportunity that whispers in our ear, "Respond now!"

When Jesus finally did arrive at Bethany, He called into the tomb and raised Lazarus's lifeless body from the dead. If you miss out on an opportunity that is truly from God because you take the time to run through the principles of God's guidance, He can raise it from the dead. God is greater than our time schedules!

Two Kings in Contrast

King David was one of those rare individuals

who did many things well: He was a skilled warrior, a talented musician and psalmist, a prophet and a deeply spiritual man. The Bible, in fact, tells us that he was a man after God's own heart. Although he was endowed with rare prophetic gifts and an intimate relationship with God, he still surrounded himself with godly counselors.

In a society that valued the role of advisors, King David is portrayed as the most consultative of all the kings in Israel's history. When making decisions, David inquired of the Lord and sought the counsel of godly advisors.

David passed this level of respect on to his sons as well. Solomon wrote numerous proverbs extolling the virtues of godly counsel. Even Absalom, David's rebellious son, understood the importance of godly counsel. Second Samuel 16:23 tells us, "Now the advice of Ahithophel, which he gave in those days, was as if one had inquired at the oracle of God. So was all the advice of Ahithophel both with David and with Absalom." David definitely consulted his advisors.

Within two generations, however, King Rehoboam abandoned the ways of his father, King Solomon, and his grandfather, King David. Second Chronicles 10 records Rehoboam's ascension to the throne upon Solomon's death. The people of Israel, led by Jeroboam, cautioned their new king, "Your father was a harsh man—he coerced many of us into forced labor and made us pay exorbitant

taxes because of his massive building pro-
grams. If you lighten the load, we'll follow
you." Rehoboam responded by saying, "Come
back in three days, and I'll give you an answer."

Israel was primed for a king who identified
with the common person. During those three
days, Rehoboam consulted many of the advisors at his disposal. He first deliberated
with the older men who had counseled his
father, Solomon; they advised Rehoboam to
lighten up in order to win over the hearts of
his people. The younger, less experienced advisors—men who were also Rehoboam's
peers—advised him to be harsher still, to
crack the whip and show everyone who was
in charge.

On the third day Rehoboam stood before
his fellow Israelites and announced, "If you
think my father was bad, just wait until I'm
through with you. My father was a wimp compared to me. He beat you with whips, but I'll
beat you with scorpions."

Rehoboam sided with his young peers and
split the kingdom of Israel in two—only two
of the twelve tribes of Israel chose to stay
with him.

Rehoboam consulted men who told him
what he wanted to hear, people who fed
Rehoboam's pride. We're no different. Men
and women in the body of Christ today often
confide in ambitious, immature and carnal
people like themselves. They pay no attention to older, godly men and women who
have failed or who have watched others fail

and have learned something from it. Instead, they surround themselves with young, untested, ambitious, spiritually stunted men and women, thinking they'll get the best wisdom from them. They seek out people who will tell them what they want to hear rather than seeking out people who will tell them what they *need* to hear. The key isn't finding just any kind of counsel; it's finding mature, godly counsel.

FOUR QUALITIES OF A GODLY COUNSELOR

Just because a person goes to church doesn't mean he or she will give you godly counsel. Look for these four qualities in a person when you seek godly counsel.

Experience. If you need advice about marriage, common sense says to go to someone who's had fifty years of success in marriage. If you're dealing with infidelity, seek out a couple who has suffered through an affair and survived. If you're considering a career change, talk to someone who has already changed careers. People with experience can help you sort through your options and will also have a good idea of what to expect—good and bad—that will result from the decisions you make.

Expertise. Expertise refers to skill. If you need financial advice, you're better off going to someone who has money and knows how to handle it. Don't consult with someone who's broke, doesn't tithe and can't pay his bills. He can only tell you how to spend your hard-earned dollars.

Honesty. King Solomon wrote in Proverbs 27:6, "Faithful are the wounds of a friend, but the kisses of an enemy are deceitful." A friend is someone who will tell you the truth, even if it hurts. Rather than telling you what you want to hear, a good counselor tells you what you *need* to hear. When seeking out counsel, go to someone who will level with you.

Spiritual maturity. It amazes me why carnal, immature Christians in trouble gravitate to other incompetent, ambitious, carnal people. Why bother getting advice from someone who loves God less than you do?

When seeking godly counsel, four questions will help you select the kind of person God can use to speak to you.

- Does this person know the Word of God? If he or she doesn't have a thorough knowledge of Scripture, how can you expect to get godly counsel? What is your safeguard against following advice that violates sound biblical principles?

- Does this person live what he proclaims to believe? Bible knowledge alone does not guarantee godly counsel. The proof of belief is in the living. James said, "But be doers of the word, and not hearers only, deceiving yourselves" (James 1:22). If you go to people who have spiritual knowledge but lack the fruit of the Spirit to back it up, you're going to people who are deceiving themselves. If their advice doesn't work for them, why would it work for you? People deceive themselves when they equate knowing the Word of God with living it. If people don't apply the Word of God in their own lives, how can you expect them to know how to apply the Word of God in yours?

- Does this person think spiritually? This may seem like an odd question, but many sincere believers think no differently than the world does. Will the person help you explore what God is trying to work in your life? God is often operating at a deeper level than the decision you are considering. Will the person encourage you to take the selfish way out, or will you be counseled in ways that will preserve your integrity? We need counsel from people who will help us apply biblical principles to our lives.

- Does this person pray? When seeking advice, go to someone who can hear God's voice. Prayer keeps our hearts soft and our spiritual ears primed to the leading of the Spirit. Prayer is the place where we become acquainted with God's character as well as His ways.

WHO SPEAKS FOR GOD?

We seek godly counsel, but God doesn't limit Himself to using only believers to speak into our lives. God can use just about anybody or anything to give us insight and direction. Even an off-the-cuff remark from an unsaved coworker can provide grist for the Holy Spirit to nudge us in a particular direction.

When making spiritually neutral decisions unrelated to integrity, morality or ethics, non-Christians may even be the best people to consult. In legal matters I would rather go to a whiz-bang heathen lawyer than an incompetent Christian who may lose my court case. A fish sticker on the bumper of a person's car does not guarantee good advice.

So I ask you, To whom are you going for godly counsel? I believe the vast majority of Christians wouldn't be able to give one name. Seeking out godly counsel requires humility and a teachable spirit—humility, because by seeking someone out you are admitting that the other person may know something that you do not; a teachable spirit, because by going to someone else, you show that you don't know everything, but you're willing to learn and grow.

Patrick Morley, in his book *Man in the Mirror*, writes, "The number one problem of man at the close of the twentieth century is that he leads an unexamined life."[1]

People are simply unwilling to open up their lives to godly counsel, correction and rebuke. To avoid being vulnerable, we fail to reach out for help. Then when we fall, no one is there to pick us up.

Devoid of godly counsel, we take our lives into our own hands, much like a pilot flying through air space without the objective input of air traffic control. The risks of going it alone are great. But with godly counsel, we find safety and success. It may cost us time and ultimately our pride, but in the end, we preclude ourselves from a total crash and burn.

QUESTIONS FOR REFLECTION

1. When was the last time you sought godly counsel from someone? What was difficult about it? What was easy?

_____

_____

_____

2. Do you currently have a friend who will be honest with you? When was the last time you received "faithful wounds" from your friend?

_____

_____

_____

3. To whom do you go for godly counsel? What qualities draw you to this person?

_____

_____

_____

4. What decisions are you facing now in which you could benefit from godly counsel?

_____

_____

_____

_____

_____

_____

_____

7

Circumstantial Evidence

THERE'S A SUREFIRE WAY TO JEOPARDIZE YOUR airplane when coming in for a landing: Look up from the instrument panel as soon as you approach the runway and continue flying only by sight. Following this procedure has done more to cause airplane accidents than any other human error. Pilots have been known to strike the ground two miles before the runway because they misjudged their position.[1]

Flying by sight is standard operating procedure during the approach, along with monitoring the instrument panel and conferring with air traffic control. But flying by sight fails miserably when it is relied upon as the sole means of navigation.

Circumstantial evidence acts in much the same way. Although helpful, it fails miserably

111

when it becomes our only means of making decisions.

Fifteen years working in human resources for a major telecommunications company merited Joel his own office and a modest income. Although he knew there was a ceiling as to how far he could rise in the company, Joel was reasonably satisfied with his work environment. He was involved in an office Bible study, many of his coworkers were people he considered friends and the atmosphere was fairly relaxed.

Occasionally, Joel conducted customer service seminars for clients of his company. Joel was surprised, however, when he was asked to conduct his customer service seminar for the investment company where Ken, his roommate from college, served as president. This firm was not a client of his company, so Joel would be acting as a consultant who would be paid generously.

The seminar ran quite smoothly, and it was good for Joel to spend a little time with Ken again, even though Ken had a temper. During the ride back to the airport for his flight home, Ken asked Joel, "Would you ever be interested in working for our firm again?"

"Of course I would," he responded without hesitation.

Two weeks later Joel came home from work and heard this message on his answering machine: "Joel, this is Ken. Hey, would you return my call as soon as you can? We'd like to fly you and Lisa back to Minneapolis for a weekend so we can discuss with you the possibility serving as our new vice president of human resources."

Joel and his wife, Lisa, flew out to Minneapolis for a weekend of wining and dining. The salary package Joel was offered was quite generous. In fact, Joel's income would be higher than he had ever dreamed he could make in human resources. The downside, however, was that he would be working directly with Ken. Joel was fully aware of his former roommate's shortcomings. Although a professing Christian, Ken's strong temper and weak sense of ethics were the reasons why the investment company was looking for someone to head up human resources—the last person quit after one of Ken's outbursts.

But Joel knew better than anyone else how to deal with Ken. *How bad could it get?* Joel thought to himself. *He wouldn't treat his old college roommate like he did the last guy.*

What would *you* do? Would you stay in a dead-end, albeit fulfilling, job with relative security, a nice pension and a modest income? Or would you choose unlimited challenges, a substantial jump in salary and the risk of jeopardizing your job security—and even more so, a friendship? Conflicting circumstances add stress to already difficult decisions.

The word *circumstance* is composed of two parts: *circum,* meaning "around," and *stance,* meaning "to stand." Circumstances, then, are those events that stand around or surround our lives. They concern our five senses: what

113

we can see, touch, smell, hear and taste. Although directly affecting our lives, they often are beyond our control.

Circumstantial evidence is the most suspect of the seven principles of God's guidance. Making decisions based on circumstantial evidence requires extreme caution. In fact, I never recommend anyone making a decision based solely on their circumstances. But God does use circumstances as one of His seven guiding principles. This is the most difficult to interpret correctly because no easy-to-explain formulas guarantee success. Circumstances can be very deceiving, as we will discover in the story of Balaam.

Lessons From a Donkey

Numbers 22 offers insight into how God uses circumstances to give us direction.

During their trek across the wilderness into the Promised Land, Israel had just conquered the Amorites and now was threatening the Moabites. Alarmed that their very existence could be at stake, the king of the Moabites, Balak, sent for Balaam, a prophet known for his powers in pronouncing blessings and curses. His commission: Curse the children of Israel so Moab would not be annihilated.

At first, Balaam refused the invitation. But after greater encouragement from Balak's emissaries, and after being granted a release from God, Balaam agreed to travel to Moab.

His one provision was that he would only pronounce what God had instructed him.

Interestingly enough, we read that although God gave Balaam the release to travel to Moab, God was still angry:

> Balaam got up in the morning, saddled his donkey and went with the princes of Moab. But God was very angry when he went.
>
> —NUMBERS 22:21–22, NIV

This brief passage gives us a glimpse into the heart and mind of God. Often God will allow us to move ahead in our own desires, even if it displeases and angers Him. At times God will answer our insistent prayers, not because it is His will, but because it is our will. But then He says, "I'll give you what you want, even if it means you eventually choke on it." Sometimes the worst thing that can happen to us is for God to answer our prayers.

So Balaam left on his journey to Moab. As he and his two servants rounded a bend in the road, his donkey came to a complete halt. The donkey had seen, standing in the middle of the road, the angel of the Lord with his sword drawn and ready to strike. Rather than risk losing its life or the lives of the other people in the caravan, the donkey turned into an adjacent field.

Balaam, unable to see what his donkey was seeing, struck the donkey to get it back on the road. This time, the donkey crossed the

115

road and crushed Balaam's foot against a wall on the other side. Like a good, loving master, Balaam responded by striking it again.

Balaam, not his donkey, should have seen the angel of the Lord. As a seer, Balaam was tuned into the spiritual realm and should have identified the angel of the Lord already. Most Bible scholars believe that Balaam didn't see what was in front of him because he was too distracted by the potential rewards King Balak had offered him for cursing Israel.

The angel of the Lord continued blocking Balaam's path, so the donkey finally gave up and laid down—on Balaam. Enraged, Balaam beat his donkey repeatedly.

At that point God opened the donkey's mouth, and the donkey spoke to Balaam, "What have I done to deserve a beating like this?"

Balaam, without the conscious realization that he was talking to a donkey, retorted, "You've made me look like a fool. In fact, if I had a sword in my hand, I would kill you right now."

So the animal, uncommonly wise for a donkey, responded, "We've been together a long time. I've been good to you. Have I ever done something like this to you before?"

"No," Balaam answered back.

Then Balaam's eyes were opened, and he saw the angel of the Lord standing before him with his sword poised, ready to strike. Out of deep reverence and awe, this highly respected man among his people fell on his face before the angel. The angel then asked, "Why did you beat your donkey? If it weren't for it, I would have already killed you by now. I came to prevent you from going any further because you were going for the wrong reasons. Had you continued, I would have struck you dead, but your donkey turned away from me three times. You, a prophet, weren't able to see what even your donkey could see."

"Forgive me," Balaam replied, "for I have sinned." He offered to return to Midian, but the angel instructed him to continue on his journey. Eventually, Balaam pronounced a blessing on the children of Israel.

We can learn five lessons from this story that shed light on the role circumstances play in the decision-making process.

Lesson #1: Never make a decision based solely on circumstances.

King Balak gave Balaam what appeared to be an offer he couldn't refuse. All he needed to do was take a little trip to Moab, curse a group of people he had never seen before, get paid a hefty sum of money and go home. Sounds fair enough. Many Christians given the same opportunity would respond, "Look how God has thrown open the floodgates of heaven. This must be the will of God!"

But our perspective reveals that by following through with the invitation, Balaam found himself resisting God. All too often, we judge an opportunity by its appearance; if it looks good, we assume it comes from God.

But committing to it would be resisting God.

After the fall of a popular televangelist in the late 1980s, the young woman caught in the middle of it all was distraught. Not knowing what to do or where to go following the shame and embarrassment from her widely publicized tryst with the former television evangelist, she sought God for direction. Soon thereafter, a popular pornographic magazine offered her a large sum of money to pose nude. Later, she commented on her "answer" to prayer and said that she had spoken with God and asked for a miracle; when the magazine called the next day, she saw that as her miracle. She then encouraged others to not give up hope, just to look up—that's where their source and strength are.

Solely based on circumstantial evidence, the pornographic magazine's offer appeared to be a blessing from God—a fat check, the admiration of men all across the country and lots of exposure! But when judged by scriptural confirmation, the offer fails. The Bible exhorts us to present our bodies as living sacrifices to God, not as objects of lust before the eyes of a bunch of dirty old men.

This also goes to show that the first open door may not be a part of God's plan. Yet that's the way many Christians perceive God's direction—they jump on the first opportunity that looks like a way out and assume it's from God. Their own impatience precludes them from experiencing God's best.

Lesson #2: God can use circumstances in seemingly contradictory ways.

As I mentioned earlier, circumstances can be very deceiving. Though the problems Balaam experienced with his donkey seemed bad to him, they actually saved his life. Had the donkey kept on walking down the road, Balaam would have been slain by the angel of the Lord. Circumstances alone are not an effective gauge in determining God's will.

When making a decision, some people comment, "All the doors were open, so I knew it was God." Well, I've walked through some open doors and then fell into holes in the floor on the other side. Other people explain, "All the doors were closed, so I knew it *wasn't* God." But occasionally God instructs us to kick the door down. Sometimes the circumstances speak to us; at other times God tells us to speak to our circumstances. The difficulty lies in discerning which way to respond.

Because God can use circumstances in seemingly contradictory ways, He can also use negative circumstances to positively affect the lives of both the righteous and the unrighteous.

God can use storms in the lives of the unrighteous to accomplish His purposes. Although the prodigal son in Luke 15 was in a storm—living in utter poverty among the pigs—he was right where God could get his attention. When God is trying to bring someone back to Himself, His will may be a pigpen or the belly

119

of a whale. God can use negative circumstances in the lives of the unrighteous in the hope of drawing them closer to Himself.

God can also use storms in the lives of the righteous to accomplish His purposes. In Acts 27 we read about a storm the apostle Paul encountered. The boat he was on sank and the cargo lost, but Paul himself escaped to the island of Malta. After he made it to land, he warmed himself by a fire. But then a poisonous snake jumped out and bit him. At that point, most people would say that God was out to get Paul. He was shipwrecked and a deadly snake bit him—there must have been some unconfessed sin in his life. And that's what the people around him assumed. But Paul was right where God wanted him to be.

Paul shook the snake off his hand. Because he showed no signs of becoming sick, the people changed their minds about him and assumed he was a god. As a result he was brought before the king, whom God healed of dysentery. Other people were also healed, and the gospel was preached. Best of all, a church was established.

Was this part of God's plan? Definitely. The detour may not have been on Paul's agenda, but it was on God's. Sometimes a detour is an interstate highway in the will of God. But He usually doesn't ask your permission to take it, or even inform you in advance.

Jesus described the work of His heavenly Father: "He makes His sun rise on the evil and on the good, and sends rain on the just and on the unjust" (Matt. 5:45). Righteous and un-righteous people alike encounter blessings and storms, which explains why obtaining guidance in the matter of circumstances de-mands maturity, wisdom, prayer, waiting on God and plenty of godly counsel.

Lesson #3: God may use circumstances to save us from future destruction.

Circumstances are like the donkey in our story. Balaam is riding his circumstances when all of a sudden, factors beyond his con-trol stop cooperating with his plans. Out of sheer frustration, Balaam starts beating his circumstances.

Notice the ascending severity in this pattern: First of all, the circumstances turned him off the road, then they crushed his foot against the wall. Finally they laid down on him. Every time Balaam beat his circumstances, they only worsened. I wonder how many times we've lashed out at the circumstances that were saving our lives? And the more we resist, the worse our circumstances get.

Circumstances at times serve as barometers into the unseen realm of God's will. Events may go wrong simply because we are moving farther and farther away from God's best for our lives. As our plans deteriorate, we be-come enraged at the very circumstances that are saving us from destruction.

A broken relationship, a canceled wedding, a lost promotion—all these may actually be acts of God's mercy. We live our lives looking forward, but we understand God's involvement in our lives when we look back. The prophet Isaiah wrote:

> The righteous pass away; the godly often die before their time. And no one seems to care or wonder why. *No one seems to understand that God is protecting them from the evil to come.*
> —ISAIAH 57:1, NLT, EMPHASIS ADDED

Even the finality of death may be an act of God's mercy to save a person from future evil. Jesus' death on a cross saved every Christian from an eternity in hell. What prevents God from allowing seemingly negative circumstances to save us from future destruction?

In his young life Joseph experienced rejection from his family, was sold into slavery and was wrongfully imprisoned. The last fourteen chapters of Genesis trace the life of a man who for years faced countless hardships. They weren't the result of a lack of faith, hidden sin or a spiritual attack. At any point he could have said, "Why am I here? God, if You love me, You will get me out of this hole they call a prison. I'm a slave; I have no rights; this is racial prejudice. I give up!"

But when his older brothers were at Joseph's mercy years later, Joseph shared with them the riches of Egypt and said, "Looking back, I can see that what you intended for evil, God meant for good. Although I have the power and authority to kill you, I won't because we all would have died had I stayed in Canaan."

Lesson #4: God may use circumstances to get our attention.

Balaam was a prophet by trade. We read in Scripture that Balaam knew the God of Israel, and he could hear God's voice. But when the time came for Balaam to change directions, his own donkey could hear God's voice better than he could. Circumstances became God's alternate means of getting Balaam's attention.

Many times we assume our employer or our spouse or a fellow brother or sister is resisting us, but that resistance might also be God. He can use the IRS to get our attention. He can even use an investigative reporter on television to speak to us. And when the circumstances finally speak, we had better listen.

Many of the well-known Christian ministers who have fallen as a result of television investigative reporting were warned, but they chose to ignore the other guidance principles. When we're unwilling to listen to godly counsel or heed the Word of God, we may be forced to listen to a donkey speak on a stage not of our own choosing. And that donkey may be clothed as a heathen reporter with a hidden camera. Airing our laundry in front of the world isn't God's desire, but He loves us enough to do it for our own good.

Lesson #5: God is more interested in maturing us than He is in delivering us from difficult circumstances.

God's ultimate plan was to demonstrate to the surrounding nations that Israel was a blessed people. And He used a Gentile to prove it.

Three Hebrew slaves—Shadrach, Meshach and Abednego—faced being thrown into a fiery furnace if they didn't bow down to the idol that King Nebuchadnezzar had constructed. Rather than seek a quick release from their difficult circumstances, they responded, "We're not going to bow down to that idol even if it means being thrown into the furnace. God will vindicate us. But even if He doesn't, we refuse to bow."

Furious because they didn't bow, King Nebuchadnezzar turned up the furnace seven times hotter than usual and had the three young men thrown in.

The ending to this story in Daniel 3 is familiar to most people. A fourth Man appeared in the furnace—the preincarnate Jesus—and the men's lives were preserved. God chose to deliver them *in* the fiery furnace, not *out of* it. The upshot of this story is that King Nebuchadnezzar converted from worshiping idols to worshiping the God of Israel. Sometimes—not all the time—allowing us to be thrown into a fiery furnace may be God's principal means of proclaiming His righteousness.

Different believers try to get around this by developing doctrines that place God in easy-to-explain categories. I'm leery of any person who has an easy explanation for why God does what He does. Scripture tells us, "For as the heavens are higher than the earth, so are My ways higher than your ways, and My thoughts than your thoughts" (Isa. 55:9).

Whenever good things happen, we sing that we are blessed. And it's true, we *are* blessed. But we place God in a box by assuming that when bad things happen, God has removed His blessing. God's purposes may be greater than the state of our personal circumstances.

Hebrews 11 describes some of the great men and women of faith as being jeered at, tortured, sawed in two, destitute and mistreated. Although they suffered in this mortal life, they died victorious. Sometimes God allows people to die prematurely. Sometimes good people who have more faith than we do suffer. Sometimes He chooses not to answer our sincere prayers of faith. His response, or lack of it, may not be the result of sin or our failure to follow the will of God. All too often we dictate to God which items we think should be at the top of His agenda. But God's goodness and faithfulness are not dependent upon whether or not He meets our expectations.

THREE KEYS FOR NAVIGATING YOUR WAY THROUGH CIRCUMSTANCES

By this point, I'm sure I have thoroughly confused you regarding how to interpret circumstantial evidence. Good. As I already

125

stated, circumstances can be very deceiving. Before concluding this chapter, allow me to give you three keys that will help you navigate your way through the murky waters of circumstances.

Avoid allowing circumstances to lead you. When we focus on the problem rather than the Problem-solver, we get confused. Even if the circumstances are positive, we must never lose focus on the God of eternity who stands behind the temporal world we see. The apostle Paul wrote, "For we walk by faith, not by sight" (2 Cor. 5:7). When I allow circumstances to determine what is good, what is bad, what is from God and what is not from God, I allow myself to be ruled by what I see. Subsequently, I place myself in the position to miss God's direction.

Avoid relying on circumstantial evidence alone. God may use circumstances to give direction, but not to the neglect of the other principles of divine guidance. Decisions grounded solely on circumstantial evidence provide an easy way out because they require no effort on our part. All we do is base our decision on what we see. But because circumstances are deceptive, walking by sight is the main reason why so many people fall on their faces after making such "easy" decisions. As we draw from the wells of Scripture, godly advice or prophetic words, we can discern the whole counsel of God.

Learn when to speak to your circumstances and when to allow your circumstances to speak to you. Crucial to making the right decision is discerning when *Satan* is opposing you because you're fulfilling the will of God and when *God* is opposing you to guard you from destruction. When you know you're in the will of God, speak to your circumstances; don't allow them to prevent you from fulfilling God's destiny for your life. But when you're unsure whether you're in the will of God or not, listen to your circumstances. They may be speaking to you as they spoke to Balaam.

Generally speaking, when we wander off the trail of God's guidance, negative circumstances escalate because the Good Shepherd is trying to nudge us back on course. At the same time, walking in the blessings of God does not preclude us from living by faith.

To plot your course through the perilous waters of circumstantial evidence, interpret your circumstances in light of the other six principles.

QUESTIONS FOR REFLECTION

1. Think about the story about Joel's job opportunity. What would you do if you were in Joel's shoes? What other guidance principles could you use to help you make your decision?

_____

_____

_____

_____

2. Remember a time when circumstances gave you conflicting messages. What finally happened? How did you determine what was of God and what wasn't?

_____

_____

_____

_____

3. Has God ever used a storm in your life to accomplish His purpose? What was your reaction at first? What do you think about the situation as you look back on it?

_____

_____

_____

_____

_____

4. Are you in any confusing circumstances now? What can you do today to gain clarity?

_____

_____

_____

_____

_____

8

The Peace of God

EVERY PILOT KNOWS WHAT EACH COLORED LIGHT on his dash stands for. There are amber lights, green lights, blue lights and a red light. When the red light starts blinking, everything else stops. The pilot doesn't worry about the comfort of the passengers or anything else. He immediately drops everything to address that red warning light because it may mean making an emergency landing or even dealing with a life-or-death situation.

If God's peace in our hearts is a green light, then that uneasiness we sometimes experience is a red light. Just as the pilot drops everything to deal with the red warning light, so we must pay equal attention to that check in our hearts.

Word of Calvary Church didn't know what to do with all the people. Since Pastor Dan's arrival five years before, the congregation seemed to have their finger on the pulse of the community. Varied ministries drew new people through the front doors of the church. Their greatest dilemma was not having enough space.

Looking to expand their facilities, Pastor Dan searched for land to purchase on the outskirts of the city. He identified a large piece of property at a prime location and negotiated with the owners—a large aerospace company—brokering a deal that looked almost too good to be true. Pastor Dan looked like a miracle worker.

One night in bed, just as Pastor Dan was almost asleep, his wife, Betty, turned to him and confessed, "You know, this land deal looks good on paper. But I must admit that inside, I just don't feel good about purchasing the property. I don't know if I feel a peace about moving ahead with it."

"What is it that makes you feel funny?" Dan answered back, trying not to sound overly defensive.

"I can't explain it. Something just tells me this isn't right."

What would you do if you were in Pastor Dan's shoes? Would you heed your wife's warning, or would you forge ahead, thinking she might be overly nervous?

God can lead us with inner peace—or the lack of it. Let's look to the Bible to discover more about God's peace.

Two Kinds of Peace

In the Bible God's peace is described in two ways: peace *with* God and the peace *of* God. Peace with God is promised to every believer. The peace of God is what He uses to guide us.

Peace with God. Paul writes, "Therefore, having been justified by faith, we have peace *with* God through our Lord Jesus Christ" (Rom. 5:1, emphasis added). Peace with God is a gift for every person who belongs to Jesus Christ.

Romans 5:10 poignantly explains the state of our relationship with God through Christ: "For if when we were enemies we were reconciled to God through the death of His Son, much more, having been reconciled, we shall be saved by His life." Before I was reconciled with God through Christ, willingly or unwillingly I was at war with God; my desires were at odds with His. I didn't think like Him or act like Him; everything I did gravitated toward self. And nothing I could do—not my good works, my charitable contributions, my perfect attendance in church—would reconcile me to God. Nothing would work except the blood of Jesus Christ. So Jesus made it possible for me to have peace with God once and forever.

The peace of God. Paul writes, "Let the peace *of* God rule in your hearts" (Col. 3:15, emphasis added). After coming to peace with God through Christ, we need the peace that comes from God. This peace then guides us

133

through the various decisions we encounter.

The Jewish understanding of peace is much broader than our understanding today. The Hebrew word for peace, *shalom*, implies more than just the absence of strife; it means wholeness, prosperity, happiness, success, security and safety. When I greet somebody and say, "Shalom," I'm not just saying, "Hi." I'm saying, "May God bless you with wholeness, health, harmony, prosperity, security and joy."

The peace of God should rule in our hearts. The Greek word for *rule* is translated literally "umpire" or "referee." During a baseball game the umpire stands behind the batter and the catcher. After the pitcher throws the ball over home plate, the umpire judges the pitch by calling "strike" or "ball." If a player on offense advances toward another base while the ball is in play, the umpire will call him either "safe" or "out." Despite the protests of players on either side, the umpire's call stands. The assumption is that the umpire represents a fair and objective judge on the baseball diamond.

In the same way, the peace of God acts as the fair and objective judge, calling the balls and strikes of our lives. When He proclaims the direction we are headed as safe, we can proceed with confidence, knowing our steps are ordered of the Lord. But when He calls a ball or an out involving a decision at hand, we must respect the fair and objective judge and not press through. His goal is not to spoil our lives, but to protect us and keep us out of bondage.

THE PEACE OF GOD IN DECISION-MAKING

God's desire is that we allow the principle of peace to umpire our decision-making. Occasionally, someone asks me for advice, and our conversation goes like this:

"I've been offered a job that pays twice what I'm making now. I'd really like to take it, but I'm not sure whether God really wants me to have it. What should I do?"

"Are you and your wife in agreement about this?"

"Yeah."

"How do you feel about it?"

"Well, I feel good; it's going to give us more security, and the benefits package is much better than the one I have now."

"Well, it looks like you have peace about it."

"Yes, we do, but we're just not sure God wants to do that for us."

Sometimes following God requires common sense. But too many believers think that the great cosmic "I AM" is just setting up a trap to trick them. "It couldn't be God; it's too good. He wants me to marry somebody who's ugly. He wants me to get a job I hate. He wants me to make less than enough."

Some folks don't know how to receive anything from God. Paul wrote that "[God] is able to do exceedingly abundantly above all that we ask or think, according to the power

135

that works in us" (Eph. 3:20). God is not only able, He's willing to surpass our wildest dreams! He is a wonderful God, and He has good purposes in mind for you. On extreme occasions something can look good and not be from God, but that's the exception, not the rule. Scripture explicitly declares that God *does* want to bless you, and He has good intentions for you.

THREE PARAMETERS OF GOD'S PEACE

The peace that comes from God doesn't just happen on its own. Romans 14:19 exhorts us to pursue peace. In any decision, relationship, business deal—whatever the endeavor—we need to pursue peace like a hunting dog hot on the trail of its prey. God uses our pursuit of peace in order to guide, govern and guard the choices we make. Let's explore those three actions of God's peace in our lives.

The peace of God guides us. What do we do when facing a decision for which Scripture gives no parameters that would indicate a *yes* or *no?* By following or pursuing peace, we allow God to use His peace to guide us.

Sometimes as we move toward a decision, we get an uneasy feeling. "I don't feel at peace about moving any further." God is using the lack of peace to say stop. Perhaps during a job search you begin negotiations with a company, then sense an overwhelming feeling of apprehension. God may be prompting you not to proceed.

Phil owned a small printing company. After his secretary quit, he hired a new office assistant, Sally, who was in her twenties and was quite attractive. One afternoon shortly after Sally began working, Phil's wife, Donna, dropped by the office. Donna discovered through the course of her conversation with Sally that she was single. She also could see by Sally's taste in clothes that she didn't leave much to a man's imagination. Knowing her husband would be spending a great deal of time alone with Sally dismayed Donna.

"Phil, you never told me your secretary was so young," Donna began.

"You never asked what she looked like."

"Did you see the way she was dressed? I don't feel good at all about you working with that woman."

"Oh, you're just jealous and insecure."

At this point, Phil's intentions might possibly be noble, but they are very short-sighted. By not listening to his wife, he reveals the heart of a fool. She has just picked up a heat-seeking missile on her radar screen. But he is ignoring her warning.

Now there isn't a wife alive who is infallible, but wives are right about 99 percent of the time. If she tells you she doesn't feel a peace about a business deal or a woman who works in the office, she's probably 100 percent right. In fact, you're safer if you just go ahead and give her the 1 percent possibility of failure, because God has wired most women with an intuitive sense that men normally won't feel.

Before moving to San Antonio to plant our church in 1984, I told God, "Until Cindy is in agreement with me, I am not moving, because a house divided against itself can't stand. If it means waiting three years until she feels a peace about moving, I'll wait, because it's not going to succeed until she's in agreement with me. We're in this together, so she needs to have peace."

Cindy did receive a peace about it, and we came into agreement. But, had we moved here against her wishes and had the church plant failed, Cindy would have had every right to say, "I told you I didn't feel good about moving to San Antonio." I would have taken the blame, and I would have been tempted to respond by saying, "If you hadn't been so negative in the first place, maybe the church *would* have succeeded." Can you see the direction the conversation would have gone? Marriages by the thousands break up because a husband forged ahead into destruction when his wife cautioned him to wait.

Whether involving a spiritual decision, a business decision or even the purchase of a car, God has given wives an intuitive sense to protect their husbands. By disregarding it, men ignore a means God has designed to guide them away from disaster and foolish decision-making.

Pursuing God's peace means we are listening to that still small voice. The peace of God will guide us—toward something or away from it—when we allow Him to be the umpire in our hearts.

The peace of God governs us. "Let the peace of God rule" (Col. 3:15). Not only does rule mean "to referee"; it can also be interpreted "to order, control or govern." We're led by God's peace, but we also allow it to govern the way we go about making decisions. Don't do anything if you are anxious or grieved in your heart.

The writer of the Book of Hebrews exhorted the readers to "pursue peace with all people" (Heb. 12:14). A person's integrity is tested when he or she refuses to proceed in a decision because the other party is not being treated fairly. Buying a home from a distressed seller may enable you to get a great deal on a beautiful place to live, but it may also leave an already troubled person in serious financial straits.

We make every effort to be at peace with others, but also, as believers, we should opt for a win-win—a decision that both parties can walk away from feeling good. As followers of Jesus Christ, we die to our own selfish desires that seek an unfair advantage over another person. That doesn't mean we shouldn't make a profit on a business deal, but it does mean we avoid unduly gouging someone because we are able to manipulate them in our favor.

Sometimes you have to fight for peace because each side will work for themselves rather than pursue what is fair for both.

Pursuing peace doesn't mean taking the path of least resistance; it means doing what is healthy and fair.

The peace of God guards us. God's peace guides and governs, but it also guards our hearts and our minds. Paul wrote:

> Be anxious for nothing, but in everything by prayer and supplication, with thanksgiving, let your requests be made known to God; and the peace of God, which surpasses all understanding, will guard your hearts and minds through Christ Jesus.
>
> —PHILIPPIANS 4:6–7

The fruit of our prayers lies not only in the answers God gives, but in the peace He bestows as well. When we walk prayerfully though the steps of God's guidance system and come to a decision, God promises to guard our hearts and minds (our emotions and thoughts). Instead of getting anxious, we can trust God with our decisions without fear of something terrible happening. Like a soldier who guards an area from attack, God's peace guards the hearts and minds of believers, preventing anxiety from taking control.

Mark and Kathy felt it was time to move to another state where Mark would enroll in graduate school. After extensive prayer together, they both felt a peace about moving ahead. The one obstacle keeping Mark and

Kathy from moving was selling the condominium in which they lived. Although the economy in their city was at a standstill and homes were not selling, they felt a peace from God that everything would work out okay.

In his home fellowship group six weeks before he was to start school, Mark announced during prayer time, "Even though our condo hasn't sold yet, I have a peace that it's still going to close in time for me to enroll in classes on the first day of school." Everyone in the class knew there were no parties interested in their condo, and they secretly wondered whether Mark was being presumptuous.

Three weeks before moving, Mark and Kathy received two offers in a twenty-four-hour period. They closed on the condo the day before they had originally scheduled to move. God's peace had guarded Mark and Kathy from anxiety and the fear of the unknown.

The prophet Isaiah prayed, "You will keep him in perfect peace, whose mind is stayed on You, because he trusts in You" (Isa. 26:3). The peace God gives is contingent upon us prayerfully placing our trust in Him.

VIOLATING THE PEACE OF GOD

In 1 Samuel 12 Saul was crowned king of Israel. Just as the president of the United States serves as commander in chief, so Saul's job description as king included leading the

Israelite army. Two years into his reign Saul began mobilizing the Israelite troops, hoping to free his people from Philistine harassment and control. After the call was sounded, the prophet Samuel sent word to the king to wait in Gilgal seven days until he returned so he could offer a sacrifice to the Lord on Saul's behalf before going into battle.

As the days passed and the Philistine army continued to grow in numbers, Saul grew increasingly anxious. By the seventh day Samuel still hadn't arrived. Vastly outnumbered and with the Israelite troops growing progressively restless, Saul's leadership was put to the test; some of his troops were deserting him, people were questioning his ability to lead and everyone was quaking in fear.

In order to prevent a full-blown mutiny, Saul made an executive decision to violate Samuel's directive and offer a sacrifice to God in his place. In doing so, Saul violated the law of God that said only the priest could offer a sacrifice to the Lord. He knew what he was doing was wrong, but he violated his peace anyway. As soon as he finished the sacrifice, Samuel arrived—on the seventh day, just as he said.

> But Samuel said, "What have you done?" And Saul said, "Because I saw that the people were scattering from me, and that you did not come within the appointed days, and that the Philistines were assembling at Michmash,

therefore I said, 'Now the Philistines
will come down against me at Gilgal,
and I have not asked the favor of the
LORD.' *So I forced myself and offered the
burnt offering.*"
—1 SAMUEL 13:11–12, NASB, EMPHASIS ADDED

What did Saul mean when he said he "forced
himself"? He had to violate the peace of God
in his heart to do what he knew he wasn't
supposed to do. He should have said, "I don't
know God's plan, but I do know God hasn't
brought us this far to destroy us. Even
though Samuel hasn't shown up and time is
running out, I'm going to wait until God directs
us to do something different."

God was testing Saul to see what was in his
heart. Because God wasn't responding in
spite of a seemingly deteriorating situation,
Saul grew anxious. Much like Saul, people
often grow apprehensive when God is silent
in the midst of increasingly stressful circumstances. But if God isn't saying anything,
then perhaps nothing is wrong. In that case,
just operate in the last word He spoke to you
until He speaks again. If I'm operating according to what God told me the last time He
spoke, then all God is saying with silence is,
"Nothing has changed. Sit down and be
quiet; all is well."

When Saul defended his conduct by
saying, "I forced myself," Samuel answered
back, "Your foolish actions have cost you the
kingdom." Now think for a minute. How many

of us at some point in our lives have faced choices, violated the peace of God and, like Saul, lost the kingdom? Romans 14:17 tells us that the kingdom of God is righteousness, peace and joy. When you violate the peace of God in your heart, you lose the kingdom—righteousness, peace and joy.

You may still have peace *with* God—the devil can't steal that because Jesus already paid for it—but he can rob you of the peace *of* God. As a result, you feel condemned and intimidated, and you wonder if God even hears or cares. Over time, people who have lost the peace of God grow increasingly distant from God.

So often, people violate the peace of God, then blame God for the loss of their peace. But through repentance, we can be restored to a right relationship and have our peace renewed. When we feel pressured or forced, when anything causes us to lose our peace, let that be a red flag from God saying, "Stop, look and listen."

WAITING FOR GOD'S PEACE

Remember that red light that gets the pilot's attention? God wants to umpire with that little red light—that sense of distress or uneasiness, that condition of lacking God's peace. I won't move forward unless my wife and I both have peace. If she doesn't feel good about it, then I'm willing to wait. If I have good facts, if I'm righteous and if God is for me, over time I'll be able to convince her. Christian or non-Christian, she'll see it.

If you're a pastor, your elders will see it. If you're a businessman, the people you relate to will see it because God guides, governs and guards with His peace. Just back off and call it quits until you get more information that brings peace.

Don't be afraid of passing up an opportunity. God will honor your obedience and willingness to be led by the Spirit. You won't wind up in a ditch. You're not going to end up in a bad relationship, marrying somebody only because you're old, desperate, lonely and with two kids.

When somebody pressures you to buy a particular house or to borrow money to invest in their business, and the situation starts robbing you of your peace, stop. You're not going to hear God and you're not going to make a right decision in an atmosphere of pressure. God doesn't operate in an atmosphere of pressure, but of peace.

If God is in it, everything will line up. If it doesn't line up, then wait. If you don't wait, you may feel as if you'll lose the kingdom; but if you do wait, God will promote you because you have passed the test.

Most North Americans don't like to wait for anything. We like fast food, fast cars—we even like our break-fast. If you feel rushed into a decision—you don't have time to get counsel or talk to your spouse about it—let it go. God won't forget you. He'll reward your willingness to wait if you heed the little red light.

Paul wrote to the Corinthians that "God is not the author of confusion but of peace" (1 Cor. 14:33). Whenever you feel confused, hurried or in disarray regarding a decision, be warned you may be rushing in where angels fear to tread because our God personifies peace.

TWO ENEMIES OF PEACE

Strife. God's desire for us is to be at peace with ourselves, our spouses, our church leaders and our coworkers. Strife is an enemy to that peace.

When we allow strife to enter into our marriage, a board meeting, a business or the church staff, the enemy then has a free door of access to come in and rob everybody's peace. Instead of peace we find confusion, accusation, stress, strife and every evil work. We need to pursue peace by eliminating unnecessary strife.

Distraction. Have you ever noticed that when things get too noisy, when you're arguing with one of the kids, when the phone is ringing and the television is too loud, it's hard to hear God's voice? You can't hear God with distractions all around. God isn't pushy; He won't vie for attention with other things. We must quiet ourselves to hear Him.

First Kings 19 tells us that Elijah was on the run from wicked Queen Jezebel. He knew his life was on the line; if he didn't get direction from God, she would track him down and have him killed. While sleeping in a cave, Elijah, tired and distraught, encountered the presence of God. Beckoned to get up, Elijah walked to the entrance of the cave and waited for God to speak.

He first withstood a fierce windstorm, but God wasn't in it. He then experienced a tremendous earthquake, but God's voice was strangely silent. Next, he faced a blazing fire, but God's presence was missing.

Then Elijah heard what seemed to be a gentle whisper. It was God's still, small voice. As God spoke, He poured His life-giving presence into Elijah, giving him a new vision for the future.

Often we don't hear God's voice because we fail to walk in the peace of God. Living at a harried pace prevents us from hearing God's still, small voice. Walking in the peace of God means turning down the volume of those things that distract us from sensing God's direction.

Watching out for these two enemies of strife and distraction enables us to be guided, governed and guarded by God's peace. So shut out unbelief, strife, confusion and the distractions this world has to offer because God works in an atmosphere of peace.

QUESTIONS FOR REFLECTION

1. How would you respond to the opening story of Pastor Dan and Betty? How do you react when your spouse has a check in his or her spirit regarding something about which you feel fine?

_____

_____

_____

_____

2. Do you have peace in your heart today? Why or why not? What can you change in your life to keep the peace of God in your heart?

_____

_____

_____

_____

3. How does strife rob you of your peace? What distractions have power in your life? What can you do today to reduce the influence of strife and distractions in your life?

_____

_____

_____

_____

_____

9

Provision

YOU HAVE BOARDED AN AIRPLANE IN NEW YORK City bound for London, England. Two and a half hours into the flight, this announcement comes over the loudspeaker:

> May I have your attention, please. We regret to inform you that before taking off from Kennedy Airport, we forgot to refuel. At the present time we do not have enough resources to complete our flight as planned. We have no choice but to return to New York City, where we will refuel and then proceed again on our flight. Your intended arrival time will be delayed by six hours. We apologize for any inconvenience this may cause you.

You understand that if the airplane had proceeded along as originally planned, it would have run out of fuel over the ocean and crashed. But what kind of confidence would you have in a pilot who failed to ensure that the plane had enough fuel before beginning the journey? Probably not much.

In our final principle of God's guidance we will examine the most practical means of determining God's direction: provision. Provision functions much like the resources at the disposal of a pilot. Before proceeding on a journey—regardless of distance—the pilot must be confident his airplane has the fuel and capability to complete the trip as planned. If lacking adequate resources to finish the journey, the passengers as well as those at the controls place themselves at great risk. Believers who make major decisions without adequate resources in place open themselves up to similar risk. Of the seven principles we explore in this book, none serve as clear an indicator of God's guidance as provision.

THE GOD OF PROVISION

An all-time favorite scripture for both Christians and non-Christians alike is the Twenty-third Psalm. The Living Bible expresses the first verse with unusual clarity: "Because the Lord is my Shepherd, I have everything I need!" God's nature is to provide for our every need. Even when we walk through the valley of the shadow of death, we can fear no evil because our God is a God of provision.

When God led the children of Israel through the wilderness, He sent manna from heaven for food. As the people grew tired of manna, he sent them an enormous flock of quail. When the people grumbled because they were thirsty, God provided a gigantic rock from which Moses drew water. God desires to provide for His people.

The Bible has hundreds of examples of God's provision. Let's look at one of the greatest—the story of Abraham and Isaac in Genesis 22.

God instructed Abraham to travel to the region of Moriah, where he would sacrifice his son, Isaac. Without so much as a fuss Abraham woke up early the next morning and packed his bags, taking with him two servants and his only son. As they approached their destination, the two left the servants behind with their supplies and continued their trek. Young Isaac, walking beside his father, asked, "We have fire and wood, but where is the lamb for the sacrifice?"

"God Himself will provide the lamb for our burnt offering," Abraham answered back.

When they reached the place God had shown Abraham, he built the altar, arranged the wood and laid his only son on top of it. Just as Abraham was poised to strike Isaac in the chest, an angel of the Lord stopped him and said, "Do not lay your hand on the lad, or do anything to him; for now I know that you fear God, since you have not withheld your son, your only son, from Me" (v. 12). At that very moment, Abraham looked up and discovered a ram trapped in a thicket. God provided a ram to be slain in place of Abraham's only son. Abraham named the place Jehovah-Jireh, meaning "The Lord will provide."

This story foreshadows the day when Jesus, almost two thousand years later, would offer Himself as the Lamb of God to purchase our salvation. God has made provision for you and me so that Jesus, the only Man who ever lived a sinless life, would die in our place, giving those who believe eternal life with God.

If God provided our means of salvation, how much more will He provide for the needs of His people? When comparing His Father's love to the intricate work in creation, Jesus said, "If that is how God clothes the grass of the field, which is here today and tomorrow is thrown into the fire, will he not much more clothe you, O you of little faith?" (Matt. 6:30, NIV). Provision is second nature to God and is useful to Him in guiding His children.

PROVISION FOLLOWS THE CALL

When God calls a person to pursue a new direction, He always works in advance of him or her. Before Jesus began His ministry God sent John the Baptist to prepare the way. Before Jesus ascended into heaven He spoke to the disciples, "I go to prepare a place for you" (John 14:2). No one ever catches God by surprise. He's always ready, and He always prepares the way for us.

When we moved to San Antonio we had no church, no salary and no support. We sold our home and made enough money to pay the bills for a short period of time. I had covered all my bases: I ran our decision through godly counsel. I had the inner conviction of the Holy Spirit and the peace of God. So I told God, "If You don't provide for our needs, I'll know that I missed You."

I wasn't concerned about defending my pride or covering up my mistakes. If it didn't work out, we would simply return to what we did before. There was no reason to be embarrassed or ashamed. When a wise man discovers he has missed God, he returns to the last place he knew he was in God's will. The foolish man keeps persisting, making excuses, when God hasn't called him at all.

But we were following God's call in His timing, so we didn't have to struggle when we planted our church. God provided. Now, if we still had twenty people after five years, then we'd have proof that God wasn't in it.

As a young man in Bible college, I was taught a quote from Watchman Nee, the great Chinese martyr, that said, "Provision is one of the first ways God uses of restraining His overzealous servants who are getting beyond the will of God for their lives. He jerks the rug of provision out from under them."

I knew a man once who was so sick of his job that he decided God must be calling him into the ministry. So off he went, with no

church support, no training and no account-
ability. He was determined to go on the mission field, and no one was going to get in his
way.

But once he got there, he almost starved to
death. It didn't take long for him to decide God
must be calling him home. Unfortunately, by
the time he returned he was skin and bones,
but more than that, he came home in disgrace.
That's not the way God guides His people.

God isn't looking for volunteers; He's looking
for people who will answer His call on their
lives. If you volunteer yourself for somebody
else's call, you'll starve to death because God
only promises to provide for His call to you.
When you volunteer, you're on your own. He
makes no promises. But if God is guiding
you, and you answer His call, He'll provide
everything you need.

It doesn't matter how anointed a preacher
you are or how well you move in revelation
knowledge. What matters is, Did God call you?
If He did, He'll confirm it through other people,
through finances and through some means of
success. You don't have to overexert yourself or manipulate others; you don't even
have to be cute or good. That's what's wonderful about the way God guides. Regardless
of whether you sense a call to ministry or
business, God works the same way.

Jesus said, "My yoke is easy and My burden
is light" (Matt. 11:30). What He calls you to
do won't give you a hernia. It just works. It
doesn't matter how smart you are, how

many mistakes you've made in the past or
how weak and obscure you may feel; God is
able to use anyone He chooses to bless.

GUIDANCE THROUGH THE
TIMING OF PROVISION

Even if you sense God calling you to make a
move, timing is still crucial. I once heard
Ralph Mahoney, the founder of the mission
organization World Map, talk about jumping
into the ministry prematurely. "For twelve
years God jerked the rug out from under me.
He kept me so poor I couldn't buy a ten-cent
trolley ticket across town. But when God's
timing came for me, He provided." Ralph
sensed the call, but God was saying, "Not yet."

Today, God uses Ralph Mahoney to release
millions of dollars into world missions. It's
interesting, though, that he couldn't get a
dime for his ministry until his calling met
with God's timing. He tried to move prematurely, but God dried up the well. If your
well is dried up, either God is moving you on
and the timing isn't right just yet, or you
missed God and you're not where you're supposed to be—because where God guides, He
provides.

GOD PROVIDES IN HIS WAY—NOT OURS

In the previous chapter we explored the story
of Elijah when he heard God's still, small
voice. Leading up to his encounter with God,

157

the prophet Elijah had pronounced a drought over Israel prompted by the wickedness of King Ahab and his wife, Jezebel. God then sent Elijah to a remote brook near Jericho, secure from the wrath of the king and queen.

> So he went and did according to the word of the LORD, for he went and stayed by the Brook Cherith, which flows into the Jordan. The ravens brought him bread and meat in the morning, and bread and meat in the evening; and he drank from the brook.
> —1 KINGS 17:5–6

Elijah knew God had called him to this obscure place because his needs were being met there. But notice the means God used to keep Elijah alive—He used ravens to bring food. According to Jewish law, a raven is an unclean bird. People in Jewish society were discouraged from touching anything unclean because by touching it, the person became unclean.

You can miss your blessing if you reject the container it comes in. God's provision may not come in a Christian container; it may not even come in a container you expect, prefer or feel comfortable with. But it's as much from God as if Billy Graham sent you a check. Just as God used a donkey to speak to Balaam, He is free to use any heathen He wants to provide for our needs. God's provision may even come in the form of a federal government program or a person who is utterly repulsive to you.

Some Christians won't listen to anyone who is against speaking in tongues and the gifts of the Holy Spirit. Other people refuse to listen to anyone who believes in these gifts. We're so afraid of anyone who may be too liberal or too fundamentalist that we end up bypassing God's word for our lives. Don't reject the blessing of God because you're judging the messenger who's bringing it. Sometimes when watching television, it's easy to say, "How can God use that preacher on television? He's strange." Well, He used a raven, and He can use that person, too.

What kind of food do you think the raven brought to Elijah? Do you think the raven delivered to him a Happy Meal? Of course not. It was probably road kill from some chariot that Elijah then cooked over a fire. Most likely it wasn't a dish he would have preferred. But it was God's provision.

WHEN GOD'S PROVISION DRIES UP

Elijah was led into in the middle of a wilderness; there God met his needs. But then the brook dried up. That's significant, because where God guides, He provides; only now His water supply disappeared.

When your resources dry up, God may be trying to move you on. Elijah's food and water were provided; he was relatively comfortable; he wasn't planning on going anywhere. Why would he? While the rest of Israel was suffering through a famine, Elijah had everything he needed. So why did God dry up the brook? To move Elijah on.

The brook dried up, then God spoke to Elijah, "Arise, go to Zarephath, which belongs to Sidon, and dwell there. See, I have commanded a widow there to provide for you" (1 Kings 17:9). What was the widow going to do for Elijah? She was going to provide for him.

"So he arose, and he went to Zarephath. And when he came to the gate of the city, indeed a widow was there" (v. 10). Elijah obeyed, and God confirmed His word again with provision.

Just because your resources have dried up doesn't mean you're under an attack from the devil. Yes, sometimes the devil is attacking you or your business, and you need to go to battle. At other times *you* may be at fault. Perhaps you allowed your discipline to slip; maybe you've been a poor manager or administrator. Once you fix the problem, the resources might start flowing again.

Identifying whether the devil is attacking you or whether God is cutting off your resources makes a big difference in how you respond. Using the seven principles of God's guidance will help you discern the difference between the two.

But sometimes it is God drying up the brook because He's giving you new marching orders. God used provision to confirm to Elijah that he was in the right place. Now as God prepares

Elijah for further guidance, He takes the provision away.

God uses provision a little like the carrot on the end of a stick that the donkey continually follows because he's trying to reach it. We follow where His provision leads us. We don't base decisions solely on income, but provision does play a key role in God's sevenfold guidance system.

The good shepherd leads the flock to green pastures, but when the immediate area has been eaten bare, the shepherd may have to move the flock over some pretty rough terrain to find the next feeding area.

Losing your job due to corporate downsizing may simply mean God has a better job for you. God didn't promise to keep IBM forever; He promised to keep you forever. So if you get laid off, there's no need to be upset or worried about your pension because God has something better for you.

What God did then, He still does today. God declares, "For I am the LORD, I change not" (Mal. 3:6, KJV). We read in Hebrews 13:8, "Jesus Christ is the same yesterday, today, and forever." If He's the same yesterday, today and forever, then God is the same Provider today that He was in the Old Testament.

FAMILY—OUR FIRST RESPONSIBILITY

A husband's primary concern when considering a decision is his responsibility to provide for his family. Paul wrote to Timothy, "But if anyone does not provide for his own, and especially for those of his household, he has denied the faith and is worse than an unbeliever" (1 Tim. 5:8). If I make a faith jump and the finances are not coming in, I had better get a job that pays the bills. That's not a sin; I'm not acting in unbelief by seeking additional employment. If my wife and children are going without as a result of the decisions I make, God says that I am *worse* than an unbeliever. The husband is accountable to God to do what it takes to provide for his family. Doing what it takes means nothing is beneath my dignity, whether that means working at a burger joint or scrubbing toilets.

Our church refuses to help men who allow their families to suffer because certain jobs are beneath their dignity. When a family is living at subsistence level, we no longer question the man's faith; we question his pride. How can we discriminate against any kind of a job if it provides for our family? More important than pursuing the dream is taking responsibility to pay the bills.

Paul told the Thessalonians, "For even when we were with you, we commanded you this: If anyone will not work, neither shall he eat" (2 Thess. 3:10). If a man refuses to work, don't bail him out or put him on benevolence; make him get a job—any kind of job that pays the bills. Of course, this does not apply to people who have disabilities and are physically unable to work.

Even the apostle Paul, the greatest Christian leader in the history of the church, worked occasionally as a tentmaker to supplement his ministry. Many of the churches he planted in Europe and Asia were unable to completely support his work. Holding a secular job is not a disgrace while you're starting a ministry. In fact, ministry begins in whatever setting God places you—whether secular or spiritual. Who knows, perhaps the base of your ministry might spring out of the secular job you hold.

SEEKING GOD FIRST

Faulty priorities cut off scores of God's people from His provision. Jesus said, "But seek first the kingdom of God and His righteousness, and all these things shall be added to you" (Matt. 6:33).

People seek guidance from God instead of seeking the God of guidance. There's a world of difference between the two. Many Christians want counseling, but they have no personal prayer life. They don't even want to pray; they just want to be told what to do. God to them is simply a means to an end. They seek the answer instead of the big solution, which is God Himself.

PUTTING GOD FIRST IN OUR FINANCES

"How am I going to pay for new tires? How am I going to get enough money to fund my kids' education?"

163

God answers, "Seek Me first—put Me first in your marriage, in your spiritual walk and in your finances—and I will provide. You'll get your bonus. You'll have your breakthrough. I'll give your child a sponsorship. I'll do whatever it takes."

God doesn't promise an opulent lifestyle, but Jesus said, "I have come that they may have life, and that they may have it more abundantly" (John 10:10). He didn't say, "I came to give you poverty." He said, "I came to give you an abundant life." That includes having more than enough to get by.

In order to seek God's kingdom first, we must honor Him in every area of our lives. And when you stop to think about it, our lives belong to Him anyway.

A specific area in which people struggle to place God first is finances. Many Christians ask God for blessings and are robbing God at the same time. God spoke through the prophet Malachi:

> "Will a man rob God? Yet you have robbed Me! But you say, 'In what way have we robbed You?' In tithes and offerings. You are cursed with a curse, for you have robbed Me, even this whole nation. Bring all the tithes into the storehouse, that there may be food in My house, and try Me now in this," says the LORD of hosts, "if I will not open for you the windows of heaven and pour out for you such blessing that

there will not be room enough to receive it."

—MALACHI 3:8–10

You may think you've done everything right, but you may unknowingly be holding back from God. By not tithing—not giving 10 percent of your income to God—you are actually robbing God and cutting yourself off from His blessing. If you're looking for God to guide you using His provision but you're not obeying Him in this, you're bringing your family, your business, even your church into a place of vulnerability.

PUTTING GOD FIRST IN OUR LIVES

Paul writes:

I beseech you therefore, brethren, by the mercies of God, that you present your bodies a living sacrifice, holy, acceptable to God, which is your reasonable service. And do not be conformed to this world, but be transformed by the renewing of your mind, that you may prove what is that good and acceptable and perfect will of God.

—ROMANS 12:1–2

Here's the deal God makes: "You give Me your body, you give Me your mind, you give Me your resources, you put Me first." If you obey this spiritual law, you'll always be able to prove the will of God. You won't miss God.

The person putting God first in every area of his life is not going to fall in a ditch. He'll be the head and not the tail. That's a promise.

When you're putting the Lord first you won't wind up in confusion. He'll give you so much confirmation that you'll have no doubts. Paul writes, "You'll be able to *prove* the will of God." But the condition is, you have to make Him your highest priority.

Is He first on every day of the week or only on Sundays? Is He first in the good times as well as the bad? Is He truly the Lord of your life? Have you accepted His forgiveness of sin through Christ Jesus as Lord? Are you giving Him His rightful place? Are you renewing your mind in His Word?

PROVISION FOR EVERYTHING

God has made provision for everything. If you're sick, He's provided healing. If you're discouraged, He's provided hope. If you're troubled and afflicted, He's the God of all comfort. If you're sorrowful, He's provided joy. If you're broke, He's made provision. He gives strength for your weakness, wisdom for your confusion and light for your darkness. He is the Provider—that's His nature as Abba Father, the God who provides for all our needs.

As we remove the obstacles that hinder God's blessing on our lives and as we submit completely to His rule and reign, we will see God use provision to guide us in the decisions we make.

QUESTIONS FOR REFLECTION

1. In what areas of your life do you know God as Jehovah-Jireh, the Lord who provides? Which time of God's provision in your life stands out the most to you? Why?

_____

_____

_____

2. Has God ever used provision (or the lack of it) to guide you in a decision? What happened?

_____

_____

_____

3. Has God ever provided for you through an unlikely source? Which source? How did you respond?

_____

_____

_____

4. What are some examples of sources God might send that Christians might easily reject? What would God's purpose be in sending us blessings in seemingly unclean containers?

_____

_____

_____

_____

_____

5. Are you giving to God financially? Is there any area in your heart or mind that hesitates in this giving? Why? What can you do today to remedy that?

_____

_____

_____

_____

_____

6. Are there any areas of your life in which you are not seeking God first? Pick one and examine it now. Why isn't God first? What obstacles are coming between you and God in this area? What one thing can you do today to change this?

_____

_____

_____

_____

_____

Part III:

The Smooth Landing

10

Overcoming Trials

FLYING INTO DENVER VIRTUALLY GUARANTEES AT some point in the flight a degree of turbulence. The phenomenon of winds blowing off the Rocky Mountains onto the plains below creates potentially dangerous conditions for even the most experienced pilot.

Turbulence is most easily explained as a contrary or circular motion of air in the atmosphere that interrupts the flow of the main wind current. If you have ever gone whitewater rafting on a river, you probably passed eddies in the water where debris and even rafts could get stuck. The same phenomenon happens in the atmosphere, where wind currents create pockets of dead air or sudden bursts of wind contrary to normal air flow. The big difference is that planes don't float on the air the way rafts do on the river.

Planes crash regularly because turbulence caught unsuspecting pilots by surprise.

Turbulence is especially dangerous during takeoffs and landings. When you're cruising at twenty-eight thousand feet and turbulence drops you one thousand feet, you have plenty of room for correction. But if you encounter a microburst as you're coming in on your approach, the strong downdraft can drive you right into the ground.

Certain indications may signal an oncoming air disturbance, such as a thunderstorm or a change in air temperature. But you really never know when one will hit until you're already in the middle of it. Even a cloudless sky is no guarantee against a sudden microburst. When turbulence strikes, anything inside the plane that isn't battened down quickly becomes an airborne projectile soaring toward an unprotected head. Pilots have been knocked unconscious when hit by a flying object during turbulent weather.

Decision-making can be turbulent as well. You may sense that God is leading you to take a step of faith. Then, after weighing your options and jumping through all the hoops, turbulence shows its fist and strikes a blow as you approach the runway. Your finances fall through, people back out, a potential buyer gets cold feet. What do you do? Do you turn around and go back? What if you're already past the point of no return? How do you make godly decisions when all hell breaks loose—the kids are screaming, the dog is barking and your world suddenly starts falling apart?

TRIALS ARE NORMAL

Turbulence is part and parcel of nearly every flight. The best way to fare through severe wind conditions is to anticipate them. Rarely does a person make a major decision without something going haywire. Without sounding pessimistic, we're better off expecting the worst and hoping for the best.

Nowhere in Scripture does God promise us that belonging to Jesus means we are inoculated against problems, that from here on out everything will turn out roses. Without a test of our faith, we wouldn't need the Holy Spirit, and we wouldn't grow.

> My brethren, count it all joy when you fall into various trials, knowing that the testing of your faith produces patience. But let patience have its perfect work, that you may be perfect and complete, lacking nothing.
>
> —JAMES 1:2–4

James encourages the reader to count it all joy *when,* not *if,* trials come. People who assume they're immune to trials become bitter when trials come because they feel God has let them down. Facing hardships is not a question of if, but of when—no matter how old or mature you are.

Not only are we to endure trials, but James also encourages us to "count it all joy." What's wrong with him? How in the world is a person supposed to be happy when trials come? We can count it all joy because of the fruit God will produce in our lives as a result of the turbulence we encounter.

TRIALS STRENGTHEN US

The state of our maturity may be of more importance to God than the outcome of our decisions. One crucial component of our maturity is the development of what the New King James Version renders in James 1:3 as "patience." In the original Greek language, the word for *patience, hypomone* is best translated "courageous endurance" or "perseverance."[1]

This word is different from the word for *patience* listed among the fruit of the Spirit in Galatians 5:22, which means "long-suffering"— putting up with a turbulent storm until it resides. *Hypomone,* on the other hand, implies patience plus a measure of resistance, enabling the person to succeed against any type of opposition.

Nothing builds perseverance like resistance. Palm trees dot many roads and provide characteristic backdrops for the beautiful vistas of Southern California. In the fifties, sixties and seventies, people flocked to this mainland paradise because of its mild climate. Temperatures seldom drop below freezing, and severe weather is rare. People seem willing to suffer through an occasional earthquake in order to enjoy the Southern California sun.

But because palm trees seldom face any sort of resistance, their root systems tend to be shallow. When a rare windstorm does arise, they topple over. At times, palm trees will fall over simply because the root system cannot support the weight of the tree.

We are like palm trees. Without opposition, our root systems tend to be very shallow. Then, when a severe problem hits, we aren't able to withstand the pressure.

God loves us too much to allow us to stay the way we are. The decisions we make and the ensuing transitions that accompany them may not be the only work God is doing in our lives. His ultimate goal is to make us mature and complete.

The New Living Translation offers a refreshing perspective on James 1:2–4:

> Dear brothers and sisters, whenever trouble comes your way, let it be an opportunity for joy. For when your faith is tested, your endurance has a chance to grow. So let it grow, for when your endurance is fully developed, you will be strong in character and ready for anything.

God may be trying to use an adverse situation to strengthen us, just as a weightlifter is strengthened by working against weights. As

I mentioned earlier, the testing of our faith produces courageous endurance, which makes us stronger. Either way, if we respond correctly, we can't lose when facing a storm.

TRIALS CAUSE US TO EXAMINE OURSELVES

So, we should expect storms to arise. When they do, our attitude toward them is crucial. When faced with turbulence many people either give up or try to force something God may be trying to stop.

Storms can be very helpful. Have you ever been so busy you didn't have time to wash a dirty car? There's nothing like a good storm to rinse it off on the way to work. Storm clouds on the horizon can also force us back to our knees in prayer to seek God regarding the presence of any sin in our lives.

Upon entering the Promised Land Joshua and the children of Israel conquered Jericho in an overwhelming victory. In a surprising turn of events, Israel was defeated in their next campaign by the inhabitants of Ai, who had gained victory with little effort. Taken back, Joshua sought God to find out what was preventing Israel from fully receiving God's promise. While Joshua was in his prayer closet, God revealed to him that there was sin in the camp. Once the sin was dealt with—the sin of Achan—the people continued receiving God's promise of possessing the land.

If circumstances start falling apart at the seams, take the opportunity to examine yourself. Perhaps the blockage you are encountering is a temporary setback permitted by God to deal with certain issues in your life. This is your opportunity to allow the storms to wash away your impurities. Sometimes God will put up with certain menial sins, but as He takes us deeper into the walk of faith, He says, "I've let you play with this sin long enough. Now it's time to deal with it." Turbulence may be the only way God can get our full attention.

SURVIVING TRIALS

Before bringing this chapter to a conclusion, I want to give you three keys to help you respond correctly when you encounter turbulence.

Monitor your airspeed. If you are going too fast in an airplane, you run the risk of sustaining structural damage. If you fly too slowly, your plane may develop a gust-induced stall. Don't proceed too fast, forcing through a situation that has obstacles. If a prospective employer starts backing up a few steps, you may be perceived as pushy or demanding by unduly pressuring him for the job. Conversely, proceeding too slowly by waiting for confirmation after confirmation *ad infinitum* may allow the opportunity God has made available to you to pass you by. No worthwhile decisions were ever made that did not include some element of risk—risk that may require a degree of faith.

Go back to the basics. If things start falling apart, it might be wise to work through the seven principles of God's guidance again. Reevaluate your inner conviction; reexamine what God's Word says; secure a third or fourth opinion from a godly person you respect.

Most of all, get by yourself and seek the God of guidance. There's always the possibility you misread the situation or ventured off course. If God is in it, it won't die prematurely, and you won't have to work to keep the dream alive. If you seek God, asking Him for wisdom, you will receive it from Him generously and without finding fault, just as He promised. (See James 1:5.)

If you run into red lights the second time around, shut it down. Go back and seek God; find out what He is calling you to do. Be thankful God stopped you before you made a fatal decision. It's better to back off than to plow through a door that God has closed because you're concerned about saving face... and then to fail anyway! "God resists the proud, but gives grace to the humble" (James 4:6).

Remember, God is on your side. Remember God loves you. He's not against you; He's for you. Our loving heavenly Father spoke through the prophet Jeremiah, "'For I know the plans I have for you,' declares the LORD, 'plans to prosper you and not to harm you, plans to give you hope and a future'" (Jer. 29:11, NIV).

Even when your dream dries up and blows away, God may be using adverse circumstances to save you from tragedy down the road. Beware, however, of becoming bitter. If you get bitter, you'll become barren and cut yourself off from the blessing of God and the voice of God. During seasons of disappointment it's easy to develop a victim mentality. Feeling sorry for yourself will do nothing except reveal that you might need a little more time to mature before moving on.

If after reexamining your situation you receive clear direction from God to continue in the face of adverse circumstances, then persevere. The enemy may be trying to stop you from obeying God in order to hinder God's blessings in your life. God doesn't change His mind about a clear command, so press through until your blessing is won. Jacob wrestled all night with an angel of God to secure his blessing. You may have to wrestle, too.

FLYING ABOVE THE STORMS

Even if you seek God with all your heart and endeavor to walk in your understanding of Him and in light of His Word, you're going to experience some trials and setbacks. But remember that God is a good God. If you plotted the progress of your life on a chart, you'd see that the line would move upward over time. Periodically the line might dip, but over a span of years, you would see that your life has increasingly progressed.

181

Facing turbulence is never enjoyable—except to the few who enjoy a good challenge. That's why God gave us the Holy Spirit—to give us wisdom and strength in the face of opposition.

Questions for Reflection

1. Should Christians face fewer problems than non-Christians? Why or why not?

_____

_____

_____

_____

_____

2. How can you make a paradigm shift in your thinking about problems? Can you decide to see them as gifts from God that demonstrate He trusts you? How would this view help you?

_____

_____

_____

_____

_____

3. Are you in turbulence right now? Review your situation in light of the seven principles you learned. Did you miss God anywhere? If not, how can you use this turbulence to your advantage?

_____

_____

_____

_____

4. What did you gain from your last experience in one of the storms of life? How can that help you today?

_____

_____

_____

_____

11

Remembering These Truths

YOUR PLANE HAS LANDED AND YOU EAGERLY disembark. Joyfully you greet those who are waiting for you. You are anxious to get on with your visit. Just remember to take your luggage with you. In it is what you need for this trip.

Let's sum up some of the truths you're taking with you as you complete the journey.

Being led by the Spirit is your birthright. No Christian has to live his or her life wondering what God's will is. "For as many as are led by the Spirit of God, these are sons of God" (Rom. 8:14). If you have given the controls of your life to Jesus Christ, you are a child of God, and it is your birthright to be led by the Holy Spirit. You don't have to flounder aimlessly wondering what direction God is leading you.

God has given you the resources you need to

discern His will. If being led by the Spirit is your birthright, then He has already provided you with the resources to determine how His Spirit is guiding you. God has given you inner conviction, scriptural confirmation, prophetic corroboration, godly counsel, circumstantial evidence, His peace and His provision in order to help you discern His guidance and to guard you against making fatal mistakes.

The bigger the decision, the more witnesses you need. For the most part, people crash and burn in their decision-making not because they consult the *wrong* resources, but because they simply fail to consult *enough* resources. Basing a major decision on one facet of God's navigation system is a little like going to only one doctor when a fatal disease has been detected.

Godly decision-making invariably necessitates a faith jump. Making a decision—especially a big one—requires faith. Waiting until there is no risk before jumping is unrealistic and precludes you from living a life pleasing to God because without faith, it's impossible to please Him (Heb. 11:6). With that said, jumping without an appropriate degree of confirmation unduly exposes you to danger.

If you get off track, getting back on will require a degree of humility. Many people never recover from a foolish decision because doing so requires swallowing their pride. "God opposes the proud but gives grace to the humble" (James 4:6, NIV). You can't expect

God to bail you out if you can't even admit you have strayed off God's path.

But God does give grace to the humble, so the best way to get up is to get down. Just humble yourself and say, "Father, I've sought my own will, and I've made a mess. I'm sorry. I humble myself today and seek Your face." When you respond like that, God will put you back on track.

If you're truly seeking God, you won't venture too far off the path. Some people become paralyzed with fear because they are overly concerned about making a fatal error. If our heavenly Father is truly the *Good* Shepherd, He won't allow us to venture too far off His path of guidance. When we do stray, He will call us back. We must keep our ears attuned to His voice.

Most of all, I encourage you with this reminder:

Seek the God of guidance more than the guidance of God. If we are truly seeking first the kingdom of God, then all the details will be taken care of as well. Knowing the God of guidance often precludes us from needing to seek His direction any further. Get to know the heart of God; spend time in His presence through prayer; immerse yourself in the Word of God. Do whatever you can to "put on" the Lord Jesus. The closer you get to God, the more you know His heart for you.

The keys to successful, godly decision-making are the same as those needed for successful flying: knowledge, experience and practice. As you grow in faith and in the ways of God's guidance, you will experience the exhilarating life that flows from the walk of faith. Exhibiting faithfulness in the lesser decisions will allow God to trust you with even greater decisions, together with the fruit that accompanies them.

My prayer is that through the Holy Spirit you will be able to use these principles to stay on course, out of error, out of destruction and out of danger, so that you can make good, godly decisions. May God bless you as you navigate your way through godly decision-making.

Notes

Chapter 2
Overcoming Obstacles to God's Guidance

1. Casey Sabella, *Titanic Warning: Hearing the Voice of God in This Modern Age* (Green Forest, AR: New Leaf Press, 1994), 55.

Chapter 6
Godly Counsel

1. Patrick M. Morley, *The Man in the Mirror* (Nashville: Thomas Nelson, 1992), n.p.

Chapter 7
Circumstantial Evidence

1. Richard L. Taylor, *Instrument Flying* (New York: McGraw-Hill, 1997), 185.

Chapter 10
Overcoming Trials

1. Kittel, Gerhard and Friedrich, Gerhard, editors, *The Theological Dictionary of the New Testament,* abridged in one volume (Grand Rapids, MI: William B. Eerdmans Publishing Co., 1985), s.v. "meno."

OTHER BOOKS BY RICK GODWIN

Training for Reigning

If you want to stay in mediocrity and power-less ritual, don't read this book! You will be greatly challenged by these scriptural insights to grow into a real spiritual lifestyle, which Jesus taught for all of His disciples. Rick brings tremendous conviction, but also tremendous encouragement to be all God has called us to be.

Exposing Witchcraft in the Church

"Rick Godwin is anointed of the Lord to shake us out of our religious traditions and bring the power of the Word back into focus."

CASEY TREAT, PASTOR
CHRISTIAN FAITH CENTER
SEATTLE, WASHINGTON

Training for Reigning and *Exposing Witchcraft in the Church* are translated into other languages. For more information, contact Rick Godwin Ministries.

For additional information on audio and video tapes by Rick Godwin, please contact:

RICK GODWIN MINISTRIES
ATTN: Bookstore
14015 San Pedro Avenue
San Antonio, TX 78232-4337
Tel: 800-675-3297
Fax: 210-402-0673

OVERSEAS OFFICES FOR PRODUCT

In South Africa:
RICK GODWIN MINISTRIES
c/o Rhema Bible Church
Private Bag X3062
Randburg 2125 RSA
Tel: 011-27-11-79-23800
Fax: 011-27-11-79-36969

In Australia:
RICK GODWIN MINISTRIES
c/o Hills Christian Life Centre
P.O. Bo 1195
Castle Hill NSW 2154
Australia
Tel: 011-61-2-9899-6777
Fax: 011-61-2-9899-4591

In England/UK:
RICK GODWIN MINISTRIES
c/o Victory Christian Centre
339 Finchley Road
Hampstead, London NW3 6EP
England
Tel: 011-44-171-794-7494
Fax: 011-44-171-435-8143

RICK GODWIN MINISTRIES
c/o Christian Resources Centre
Bramble House
Bramble Street
Derby DE1 1HU
United Kingdom
Tel: 011-44-1332-367-367
Fax: 011-44-1332-201-767